Cambridge Elements

Elements in Historical Theory and Practice
edited by
Daniel Woolf
Queen's University, Ontario

HISTORY AND HERMENEUTICS

Paul Fairfield
Queen's University

Shaftesbury Road, Cambridge CB2 8EA, United Kingdom
One Liberty Plaza, 20th Floor, New York, NY 10006, USA
477 Williamstown Road, Port Melbourne, VIC 3207, Australia
314–321, 3rd Floor, Plot 3, Splendor Forum, Jasola District Centre,
New Delhi – 110025, India
103 Penang Road, #05-06/07, Visioncrest Commercial, Singapore 238467

Cambridge University Press is part of Cambridge University Press & Assessment,
a department of the University of Cambridge.

We share the University's mission to contribute to society through the pursuit of
education, learning and research at the highest international levels of excellence.

www.cambridge.org
Information on this title: www.cambridge.org/9781009607827

DOI: 10.1017/9781009607810

© Paul Fairfield 2025

This publication is in copyright. Subject to statutory exception and to the provisions
of relevant collective licensing agreements, no reproduction of any part may take
place without the written permission of Cambridge University Press & Assessment.

When citing this work, please include a reference to the DOI 10.1017/9781009607810

First published 2025

A catalogue record for this publication is available from the British Library

ISBN 978-1-009-60782-7 Hardback
ISBN 978-1-009-60778-0 Paperback
ISSN 2634-8616 (online)
ISSN 2634-8608 (print)

Cambridge University Press & Assessment has no responsibility for the persistence
or accuracy of URLs for external or third-party internet websites referred to in this
publication and does not guarantee that any content on such websites is, or will
remain, accurate or appropriate.

For EU product safety concerns, contact us at Calle de José Abascal, 56, 1°, 28003
Madrid, Spain, or email eugpsr@cambridge.org

History and Hermeneutics

Elements in Historical Theory and Practice

DOI: 10.1017/9781009607810
First published online: June 2025

Paul Fairfield
Queen's University
Author for correspondence: Paul Fairfield, paul.fairfield@queensu.ca

Abstract: Philosophical hermeneutics has shed a good deal of light both upon the methodological underpinnings of the humanities and social sciences generally and in particular upon some fundamental issues in the philosophy of history and history proper. The aim in this Element is to analyze those of its arguments that bear directly upon the latter fields. The principal topics taken up are Dilthey's distinction between understanding and explanation, the accent on meaning and experience, and the sense in which individuals may be said to belong to history. Heidegger's account of historicity and being-in-the-world, Gadamer's conceptions of historical understanding and belonging, and Ricoeur's view of historians as storytellers also come in for analysis. Other themes include the sense in which one may speak of a dialogue with the past, the notion of historical truth, and the problem of constructivism.

Keywords: theory of history, philosophy of history, historical understanding, historical truth, hermeneutics

© Paul Fairfield 2025

ISBNs: 9781009607827 (HB), 9781009607780 (PB), 9781009607810 (OC)
ISSNs: 2634-8616 (online), 2634-8608 (print)

Contents

Introduction: Hermeneutics and the Philosophy of History   1

1 Explanation and Understanding   8

2 Historical Belonging   21

3 Narrative Configuration and Prefiguration   35

4 The Constructivist Overcorrection and Other Developments   47

Bibliography   60

Introduction: Hermeneutics and the Philosophy of History

What historians do and what happens to them behind their backs are distinct questions. What they do is surely complex – pose questions, gather and sift evidence, interpret meanings, justify claims, criticize competing accounts, fashion narratives, and some other things – yet the second matter may be still more so. Historians, among the many things that they do, seek to understand what happened in the past and what it can be said to mean or to have meant, while the question of "what happens to us" in this search for understanding is at once enigmatic, philosophical, and also hermeneutical. As the foremost exponent of philosophical hermeneutics through the latter decades of the twentieth century, Hans-Georg Gadamer, expressed it in an often-quoted line: "My real concern was and is philosophic: not what we do or what we ought to do, but what happens to us over and above our wanting and doing." He might have said his primary concern, for he was hardly silent on the issue of "what we do," as he would clarify in the same text a few pages later: "I have therefore retained the term 'hermeneutics' (which the early Heidegger used) not in the sense of a methodology but as a theory of the real experience that thinking is."[1] He was speaking not only of historical thinking but of thinking or understanding in general and of what has already occurred prior to the thinker doing whatever it is that they do. The elusiveness of this second question should not be underestimated. We see what is before us, often "through a glass, darkly," but what is behind us is an elusive matter indeed. To change the metaphor, an audience witnesses the drama as it unfolds on the stage but not how the stage was set before the actors walked onto it. What has "always already" (an overused but necessary phrase) happened prior to our overt activity, whether we are speaking of historians or of intellectual investigators generally, calls for reflection if our theme is historical knowledge – what it is, what makes it possible, and what its limits are. What makes knowledge in any field of inquiry possible also conditions and limits it, usually without our awareness. The task of the philosopher of history, then, includes this setting of the stage no less than the more overt but still difficult business of understanding the drama.

Hermeneutics for well over a century now has taken up these questions in ways that the following sections seek to analyze. The premise of the present study is that philosophical hermeneutics sheds a good deal of light not only upon the methodological underpinnings of the humanities and social sciences in general – by now a familiar hypothesis – but in particular upon some fundamental issues in the fields of philosophy of history and history proper. Our aim

---

[1] Hans-Georg Gadamer, *Truth and Method*, second revised ed., trans. Joel Weinsheimer and Donald G. Marshall (New York: Bloomsbury, 2011), xxviii, xxxiii.

in what follows is not to provide a general introduction to philosophical hermeneutics but to analyze those of its main theses that relate directly to the fields just mentioned. (See the bibliography for a few such introductory texts as well as more specialized works.) An appropriate point of departure is Wilhelm Dilthey's critique at around the turn of the twentieth century of the philosophy of history of his era and the century that had preceded it. What we might call philosophy of history in the grand style had posited a universal and knowable order that had persisted through the rise and fall of civilizations and which was a kind of secular counterpart to divine providence. If Augustine in the fourth and fifth centuries can be spoken of as the founder of the philosophy of history in this sense, he was speaking of sacred or salvation history rather than profane history. The philosophy of history in the latter and now standard connotation is a modern phenomenon which may be thought of as a secularization of a much older and theological interpretation of history, and whose principal theorist is undoubtedly G. W. F. Hegel. History on this no longer theological but still teleological view has an order and a plan which a great many Enlightenment thinkers had conceptualized in the idea of progress. "From the sphere of natural science," as Dilthey noted, "with its universally valid knowledge of the lawful system of the universe, came the idea of the solidarity and progress of the human race. What religious conceptions had seen metaphorically was now the object of scientific knowledge."[2] The story of human history is of the onward march of the species away from the primitive and toward the gradual attainment of emancipation and enlightenment, culminating in the present moment but which can also be anticipated to lead toward a future apex of one kind or another. In Hegel's theory of historical development, the concept of progress found its most thoroughgoing elaboration and defence, although the concept itself was ubiquitous a century before his *Lectures on the Philosophy of History* of 1822–1830.

For Dilthey, progress itself – this most central concept of the Enlightenment – had been essentially read into the phenomena of history rather than found there as a consequence of the scientific revolution from which the idea of progress emerged. The proposition that knowledge and culture in their entirety were advancing toward a telos had a scientific veneer while being itself unscientific, for "there are no experiments that enable us to ascertain under what circumstances a historical event would not have taken place."[3] The idea of progress is unverifiable even as it passed for a couple of centuries as something of an

---

[2] Wilhelm Dilthey, *Hermeneutics and the Study of History*, Selected Works vol. IV, ed. Rudolf A. Makkreel and Frithjof Rodi, trans. Patricia Van Tuyl et al. (Princeton: Princeton University Press, 1996), 339.
[3] Ibid., 268.

History and Hermeneutics 3

orthodoxy which only the most skeptical would challenge. Dilthey's critique of it and of modern philosophy of history more broadly is essentially methodological: the method that had been employed in both German philosophy of history and French sociology amounts to a "creative intuition" of a *notio universalis*, a confused and indeterminate general representation abstracted from a mere survey of the nexus of history. It is an unscientific abstraction under whose broad cloak man's increasing control over nature converges with the growing influence of his higher capacities over his lower, of his intelligence over his passions, and of his social inclinations over his egoistic ones." Nothing about this is empirical but the veneer, as neither historians, philosophers of history, nor sociologists had discovered any such law in the evidence itself but had imposed it in a grand act of hermeneutic imposition. Progress was not the only such "unscientific abstraction"; "abstract entities such as art, science, state, society, and religion," on his view, "are like fog-banks that obstruct our view of reality" and "cannot themselves be grasped." Concepts of this kind are supposed to unlock the truth of what he would call "socio-historical life," yet their constant tendency is to obscure what they are meant to clarify.[4] The principle of teleology in particular "will never succeed" since the type of abstraction it requires soars so high above historical particulars as to lose contact with them.[5] This mode of speculation, whether we are speaking of Hegel's universal history or Auguste Comte's sociology, "completely oversteps our human power of observation." The opposite stance of what Dilthey called "the pragmatic historian" replaces universal laws with a resolute particularism where historical actors and events resemble atoms without relation or meaning, and it is no improvement over its antithesis. Both approaches "fail to understand each other" and the human past no less "because they start their discourse from two opposite perspectives: the solid earth and the ethereal heights. Yet each of them possesses a portion of the truth." The particularist and the universalist grasp elements without a richer understanding of the significance and indeed the truth of what they see. A further problem for the universalist is that history itself "no more has such an ultimate and simple message which would express its true sense than does nature"; to our knowledge there are no discernible laws for the historian to discover, and it is only the hegemony of natural science that led us to anticipate finding any in the historical world.[6] Any truth to be understood in the realm of socio-historical reality emerges from no formula but from the

---

[4] Wilhelm Dilthey, *Introduction to the Human Sciences*, Selected Works vol. I, ed. Rudolf A. Makkreel and Frithjof Rodi, trans. Michael Neville (Princeton: Princeton University Press, 1989), 153, 156, 93.
[5] Dilthey, *Hermeneutics and the Study of History*, 355.
[6] Dilthey, *Introduction to the Human Sciences*, 160, 103, 141.

undogmatic and hermeneutic art of reading particulars in relation to other particulars and within some larger context that is nothing as simple as a plan.

Phenomenological and hermeneutical thinkers in the twentieth century would follow Dilthey both in their skepticism of the philosophy of history in the grand style and in placing an accent on meaning and experience (primarily in the sense of *Erfahrung* or experience in a richer and more general connotation than *Erlebnis*). Dilthey's empirical bent issued in no simple empiricism but a phenomenological and hermeneutical concentration on the meaningful dimension of human events. Historical understanding requires a rising above the order of the chronicle to a larger configuration in which meanings can come into view, and large metaphysical constructions are not useful for this purpose. Human reality is saturated with meanings of which the search for understanding is unending, whether we be historians, philosophers, or anyone else. Our thought about this reality cannot look behind the phenomena of life itself but focusses on what is given to us in experience (*Erlebnis*), where what is given are not what empiricists had called "sensations" but meanings that are not isolated but that relate to life in its entirety. As Gadamer would later remark, since every experience "is itself within the whole of life, the whole of life is present in it too." Aesthetic experience is a case in point: the work of art is a human expression of meaning which breaks into our life at the same time that it illuminates life in its entirety. "To understand is to understand an expression," from a work of art to an historical action.[7] The human past bears meanings that continue to speak to us, and these experiences are the basic elements of historical understanding. Some larger configuration is what we seek, but nothing so large or abstract that it loses contact with those experienced meanings of which the historical past is replete. Dilthey would anticipate Edmund Husserl and the phenomenological movement's accent upon lived experiences as well as the temporality and historicity of our existence, as we shall see in the sections that follow. Human reality is not limited to the physical world but encompasses language and culture, history and art, and the larger manifold of experiences and meanings in which life is played out. The work of the historian is to navigate the complexities of this reality by configuring and reconfiguring the myriad elements of a chronicle into an intelligible account which brings us into working touch with a past that is a living past. A story that holds significance does not speak of bare particulars but relates facts and meanings to other facts and meanings and sets forth the context in which each of them occurred. The intelligibility of an event is contingent upon such relations and patterns, on its contribution to some meaningful whole which continues to bear upon the present. For Dilthey, the humanities and social sciences in general

---

[7] Gadamer, *Truth and Method*, 60, 219.

(*Geisteswissenschaften*) are engaged in a common effort to understand the socio-historical world in its various dimensions, and where such understanding is not an external imposition but an interpretation of what has taken place and what has been expressed through the ages.

The hermeneutics that is indicated in the title of our study does not carry a wholly unified connotation. The term has held different meanings through the last few centuries, and it is no exaggeration to speak of distinct hermeneutic traditions and approaches. I shall be speaking in the following sections primarily of hermeneutics or philosophical hermeneutics in the principal sense in which the term has been used since the publication in 1960 of Gadamer's magnum opus, *Truth and Method* and in that thinker's subsequent work. Historically, to make a long and complicated story short, the term and the discipline arose out of the Reformation and Counter-Reformation's effort to fashion rules by which particular biblical passages might be interpreted by clerics charged with explicating divine meaning for their congregations. A branch of theology, hermeneutics soon turned in other specialized directions such as law where again the preoccupation was pragmatic: how to bring general legal requirements to bear upon particular cases, which again involves the careful business of interpretation. Theological, legal, literary, and historical hermeneutics in the nineteenth century coalesced in the thought of Friedrich Schleiermacher and Dilthey into a general method by which texts or expressions of any kind may be validly interpreted. The search was on for a principled method or art by means of which everything intelligible becomes known in a way that is rationally defensible, and the primary fruit of this quest was what Schleiermacher termed the "hermeneutic circle." Taking a clue from Augustine, the idea here is that the interpretation of a particular text or passage is properly informed by the meaning of the text as a whole, while the meaning of the text as a whole is equally informed by particular passages in a constant process of looking back and forth at the universal and the individual. Meaning emerges from this dialectical or back-and-forth movement, and it is an idea that twentieth- and twenty-first century hermeneutical thinkers continue to uphold, somewhat less as a rule for interpretation than a phenomenological description of "what happens to us" when understanding occurs. Historical inquiry is not excepted: understanding a past event involves relating it to some larger universality, and where the larger universality ought not be conceived as a law-like regularity but something decidedly smaller in scale. As Dilthey pointed out, we are not forced to choose between an impossibly speculative universalism and a particularism so quotidian as to defy understanding.

Since the publication of *Truth and Method*, the principal connotation of hermeneutics – philosophical hermeneutics still more – is the phenomenological enterprise of describing what interpretation or understanding (approximate synonyms) is and what has taken place prior to the interpreter's explicit activity of revealing the meaning(s) of their object, be it a text, event, action, work of art, or what have you. Heidegger's thought most notably in *Being and Time* initiated a shift, carried further by Gadamer, Paul Ricoeur, and a number of more recent thinkers, away from the methodological hermeneutics of Schleiermacher and Dilthey and toward an ontological hermeneutics wherein understanding is not merely a cognitive activity in which we sometimes engage but, more fundamentally, our very mode of being-in-the-world. Regarded phenomenologically and hermeneutically, Aristotle's point that human beings bear a rational principle or logos means that we are speaking animals and that our understanding of ourselves and our world, as Gadamer expressed it, "is the original characteristic of the being of human life itself."[8] Understanding is more what we "are" than what we "do," or before any such "doing" – whether we are speaking of historical, theological, literary, or any other interpretation – we have already preunderstood our object from within our own hermeneutical situation or, as Nietzsche had said, "perspective."

The intellectual atmosphere in the early part of the twentieth century in which the ontological and phenomenological shift in hermeneutics began was broadly characterizable by a reaction against the positivism and scientism that had prevailed through a good part of the nineteenth century in disciplines ranging from philosophy and historiography to the humanities and social sciences in general. History itself which had long fallen under the umbrella of rhetoric emerged in the nineteenth century as both a profession and an empirical science whose task was to know the past "as it essentially happened," as Leopold von Ranke famously put it. The central concept was "research," in a connotation of the term that differed little from the form of knowledge belonging to the natural sciences. Historical inquiry was to be objective, value-neutral, explanatory, and no less empirical than physics or biology, or so the positivists contended. The critique of historical objectivism which Johann Gustav Droysen initiated would be extended by Nietzsche, Dilthey, and Heidegger, while the critique itself belonged to a larger project of accounting for the theoretical underpinnings of the human sciences as a whole. The latter disciplines stood in need of a Francis Bacon-like figure who could carry out for the human sciences what he had performed for natural science, which is to place them on a sound methodological basis without falling into a positivism which was appearing increasingly untenable. The method of the natural sciences is not simply transferrable to the human, Dilthey and later hermeneutical philosophers maintained, and nor are

---

[8] Ibid., 250.

the latter disciplines deficient as a result of this. Nietzsche and Dilthey were placing interpretation at the centre of philosophy and the human sciences as a whole, and it remained to work out the implications of this view for the study of history.

If philosophy of history in the grand style was no longer tenable, was it possible in any style or was it destined for the scrap heap? Neither history proper nor the philosophy of it could be placed on the secure path of science, but some critique of historical reason might yet be possible in the sense of an understanding of what historical research itself is and of what happens to us in the process of undertaking it. As Dilthey put it, "If we speak of a philosophy of history, that can only mean historical research which has a philosophical bent and makes use of philosophical resources." Research with a philosophical bent operates within the hermeneutic circle or looks back and forth from universal to particular, and to do this the historical interpreter must have some conception of the universal if we do not wish to be left in the position of the "pragmatic historian" whose bare particulars are devoid of significance. The task of the philosophy of history is to bring this larger universality into focus, and where we are not building castles in the air but identifying tendencies, dynamics, regularities, and recurring themes that are already operative in human events as we experience them. Such relative "uniformities" and "enduring phenomena" are investigated throughout the human sciences, and historical research draws upon all of them. To cite Dilthey once more, "In the historical world – which, like the sea, always moves in waves – there are enduring phenomena, such as religions, states, and the arts, which, being constituents of psychophysical interactions, represent lasting creations and as such are investigated by the particular human sciences."[9] The search for some larger understanding of the past than what the pragmatic historian makes visible begins with the recognition of the manner in which historians themselves belong to the historical world which is their constant object of investigation. We are historical beings from the ground up and thus do not hold the past at an objective distance. We understand history from within a history that has already constituted us, and there is no place outside it from which to grasp the whole. Historical understanding is internal in this sense, and any philosophy of it must accentuate themes of historical belonging, the temporality of human existence, the search for meaning, the conditions and limits of our knowledge of the past, and the hermeneutic situatedness of the historian. These are some of the themes I shall discuss in the sections that follow.

---

[9] Dilthey, *Introduction to the Human Sciences*, 141, 164.

1 Explanation and Understanding

The philosophy of history is often distinguished into two branches: the first is what I have referred to as the theory of history in the grand style which has sought a universalist model of the historical process itself and whose principal theorists have included Hegel, Marx, and the numerous exponents of progress from whom we have heard for a few centuries now; and the second concerns the nature of historical knowledge. Hermeneutical philosophers have focused on the latter and have been relatively silent on the former. Since Dilthey, this movement's primary concern has been to account phenomenologically for what form of knowledge is historical knowledge and what has already taken place behind the historian's back and how this conditions or preforms our understanding of the past. What emerges is the past "as it really was," we may still say, but with some important qualifications. Dilthey's critique affords a point of departure: universalist history has been excessively speculative and impossible to ground in the kind of evidence with which historians concern themselves. Any philosophy of history must have its feet on the ground and search not for law-like regularities but approximate patterns, recurring themes and tendencies which afford some relatively comprehensive view of the human past without transforming these into the metaphysical "fog-banks" we have seen too many times before. The task of the historian, and of the philosopher of history at a more comprehensive level of analysis, is neither to explain causes and effects nor to issue predictions but to understand meanings. Historical understanding has a circular structure whereby we move from particular to universal and back again and we are ever investigating where a trail leads, what led to a given event, what meaning can be discerned, how we can be said to know any of this, and what such knowledge amounts to.

This section focusses on two hypotheses, both of which are fundamental to a hermeneutical conception of historical inquiry. The first is Dilthey's claim that while the natural sciences seek causal explanations of natural events, the human sciences, including history, aim to understand the meanings of human expressions and actions. Dilthey's distinction between explanation, answering "why" questions, and understanding, answering questions of meaning, generates consequences for how we understand the historian's task. That task is essentially hermeneutical: to understand what a given period or set of events within it meant to the people of that time and also how it continues to speak to the present. The second claim is Gadamer's hypothesis regarding what he called the universality of hermeneutical reflection or the ubiquity of understanding and the search for it in our experience of the world in general, including our investigations of the past. Human beings, speaking ontologically, are

History and Hermeneutics 9

hermeneutic animals, that is, speaking animals who find our way about the world by means of linguistically mediated understanding. The historian is but one instance of this, and becoming aware of our hermeneutic situation – the fundamental condition in which knowers find themselves prior to overt cognitive activity of any kind – reminds us of the finitude of understanding in general and of the dubiousness of some modern conceptions of historical explanation.

We begin again with Dilthey in the latter part of the nineteenth century and the early years of the twentieth. His larger project was to achieve for the various fields of the *Geisteswissenschaften*, or the humanities and social sciences as a whole, what Bacon had achieved for the natural sciences, which is to place all of them on a sound epistemological and methodological foundation. Some of these disciplines were at a relatively early stage of development or had become newly professionalized while their intellectual underpinnings had remained questionable. Comte and the positivists, it seemed to Dilthey, had overestimated the scientificity not only of the new field of sociology but of knowledge across the disciplines, and it fell to him to carry out the rather large undertaking of providing a correction that neither posited an impossible objectivism nor flew to the opposite extreme. The dichotomy of a full-blown objectivism or subjectivism needed to be replaced by a conception of knowledge that is cross-disciplinary, methodologically sound, historically situated, and finite. Hermeneutics, in Schleiermacher's understanding of that term, seemed a promising candidate. Here was a conception of knowledge that is broadly applicable to the human or cultural world, once its details and implications could be worked out by the epistemologically minded philosopher. Such was Dilthey's task, most notably in his broad-ranging *Introduction to the Human Sciences* but beyond this in a large body of work most of which remained unpublished in his lifetime.

The question is rather expansive: how is the human scientist working in any of these fields to proceed? Which questions ought they to be asking and which exceed their grasp, and by what procedure is the whole enterprise to be conducted? Dilthey urged that we attend closely to the myriad relations that attend whatever particular elements of the human world we wish to understand. Without proposing a dichotomy between art and science or between the "hard" or natural and the human sciences, and speaking very generally, the human sciences concern themselves in the main with a field of objects that overlaps with but is importantly distinct from the natural, with a cultural and historical world that never loses contact with nature but that also transcends it. Aristotle's principle that the method of intellectual investigation depends upon the object here comes into play: the set of objects that the *Geisteswissenschaften* (a word, incidentally, which was a German translation of John Stuart Mill's rather unusual English term "moral sciences," and which is standardly translated back into English as human sciences) take up consists in the main of humanly significant meanings, expressions, and artifacts rather than naturally occurring and material objects. If the method of inquiry is in principle contingent upon its object then we may expect the methodology of the human sciences to differ in important ways from that used in the study of the natural world, and in making this move Dilthey advanced his case against positivism and for the independence of the human sciences. An historical event is no more reducible to a physical happening than a song or an emotion but bears a meaning that we are trying to bring into view. Placing it in view involves asking the right sort of questions and leaving aside those that stand in the way of our object. It is a false supposition and a lingering effect of positivism that the human studies are "soft" relative to the natural because of some deficiency in their objects. Some qualitative differences between the kinds of matter with which the natural and human sciences concern themselves do exist, and such differences immediately raise the question of a methodological division.

Here Dilthey's position is that the human sciences require a separate foundation and methodology from the natural: "we must provide an epistemological grounding of the human sciences, justify and support their independent formation, and once and for all put an end to the idea that their principles and their methods should be subordinated to those of the natural sciences." The "subject matter" in each of the human sciences "is composed of units that are given rather than inferred – units that are understandable from within. Here we start with an immediate knowledge or understanding in order to gradually attain conceptual knowledge." The hermeneutic method avoids the basic error of the positivists which is "to truncate and mutilate historical reality in order to assimilate it to the concepts and methods of the natural sciences," and instead seeks an ever-expanding integration of elements of the socio-historical world into some relatively comprehensive picture. The world we live in is no longer nature but society: "Nature is alien to us. It is a mere exterior for us without any inner life. Society is our world. We sympathetically experience the interplay of social conditions with the power of our total being." The matters into which historians inquire are not external but internal, in the sense that the historian's own standpoint and being are of the same substance as that which they are investigating. What they seek is a sympathetic understanding of what things meant for the occupants of a given time and place and to overcome the distance between past and present by re-experiencing what they experienced in whatever way is possible for us. The mode of knowledge that the natural sciences offer here is not irrelevant, but it is preliminary. The proper focus for the human scientist is upon the meaningful dimension of human experience in all its

History and Hermeneutics 11

complexity and interrelatedness to other experiences, and all through the medium of human expressions. This invariably involves taking some cultural object out of isolation and regarding it in the context of its world and the many other elements with which it bears a relation. The historian's task goes beyond "the mere gathering and sifting of material" and "encompasses the complex facts of the human world in their connectedness, as grasped in narrative history and in the statistical studies of the present." The historian seeks a solidarity with the past or an intimacy that is made possible by grasping the innumerable connections between cultural elements of both the past we are studying and the present. "The individuality and profusion of interactions that emerges here is boundless," and for this reason the historian's task is forever incomplete.[10] There is always more to understand for as long as the past events we are describing bear relations to a history that is ongoing.

Historians and other human scientists seek an understanding of their object, and we understand nothing in the socio-historical world in isolation. We require evidence and a great deal of it, and where evidence must be integrated into some intelligible configuration. Indeed, the concept of evidence already means evidence-of-X or relative to some matter that goes beyond itself such as a context or a narrative. The overriding imperative is to understand what happened, what it means or meant, how a given event came to pass, what led to what, what lasting effects it produced, and how all of this can be known. A great deal of empirical investigation is necessary for this purpose and a sifting of evidentiary material. Difficult evaluations of what is reliable and what is unduly speculative, following trails, going down rabbit holes or breaking off the chase, and making judgments all belong to the art of historical inquiry. It transcends the amassing of information to involve its synthesis, analysis, and interpretation – and where information itself, like evidence, is only ever information-about-X and nothing apart from its bearing upon some matter that we are endeavouring to understand. But what is understanding itself and from what is it distinguished? Droysen had drawn a rather sharp distinction between understanding and explanation and advanced the view that the historian properly seeks the former and not the latter. (Shortly after Droysen, neo-Kantian philosopher Wilhelm Windelband distinguished between "nomothetic" and "idiographic" knowledge, where the former connotes a generalizing tendency associated primarily with the natural sciences while the latter is oriented toward particulars and is more characteristic of the humanities, although he regarded both forms of knowledge as present in each of the disciplines.) Historians do not explain, if we mean by explanation a causal account of how

---

[10] Dilthey, *Introduction to the Human Sciences*, 158–159, 49, 88, 91, 89.

a given event came to pass. Natural scientists explain in this sense or answer "why" questions regarding our experiences of the natural world. Human scientists do not, for the reason, Droysen argued, that human beings are free and behave as agents rather than billiard balls. The motions of the latter and the entire range of phenomena with which the natural sciences concern themselves are explainable as effects of causes, more specifically what Aristotle called efficient and material causes. Human actions are voluntarily undertaken and thus are without causes in these senses of the word. While the physicist seeks to explain, the historian seeks to understand – although Dilthey would be somewhat less categorical than Droysen in drawing this distinction. What, then, is understanding?

It is not (primarily) to explain, or rather at the heart of understanding is not an accounting of causes and effects but something qualitatively different from this for the reason that "we are not blind forces but rather volitional creatures that reflectively establish their purposes."[11] We act with a purpose (Aristotle's final cause), and while that purpose is not seldom elusive, several in number, conflicting, confused, irrational, or downright pathological, we still act with a purpose. The meaning of our action relates to this purpose, and the adjectives just employed to describe human purposes apply equally to meanings. They are elusive and often exceedingly intricate, especially when we are speaking of the kind of events in which historians are interested. But they bear meanings nonetheless, and it is these that the historian seeks to understand in the sense of re-experience or "recognize, behind signs given to our senses, that psychic reality of which they are the expression.... If, for instance, I wish to understand Leonardo, my interpretation of his actions, paintings, sketches, and writings coheres as a single homogeneous and unified process."[12]

The interpretive process begins with a human being or collectivity making manifest in an outward action, artifact, or work some meaningful experience or expression of life which need not be limited to an internal state of mind. An interpreter subsequently perceives this expression and attempts to bring this within one's own consciousness or to experience again that of which the expression is an expression, be it an idea, intention, or lived experience of whatever kind. Some external manifestation of life is experienced internally in an act of imaginative empathy.

Interpretation on this view amounts to an overcoming of alienation and a re-experiencing of a meaning that is socially shared. Any object of study within the human sciences becomes known to us by comprehending together experience or what he would often call "life," expression, and understanding. Life is

---

[11] Ibid., 69.   [12] Dilthey, *Hermeneutics and the Study of History*, 236–237.

permeated with meanings which become expressed outwardly in myriad forms, from a law to an institution, a text, an action, a social movement, and so on. The work of interpretation is to grasp the rich experience of another, and it is not a purely technical form of knowledge. Whereas causal explanation is technical and intellectual, interpretation integrates the various capacities of the mind in comprehending the experience of others in its full complexity, and it is a type of knowledge that is valuable in itself. Unlike natural scientific explanations of a phenomenon which is of interest primarily for what it indicates about a general hypothesis or law, hermeneutic interpretation is not a means to something beyond itself. In each of the human sciences, we are interested in the particular and the lived experience of others for its own sake. The particular does not stand at a radical distance from us and may be entered into with a relatively full knowledge of the context in which it occurs. To understand it means to grasp it from the inside, as it were, or as the subject experienced it to whatever extent this is possible. The historian imaginatively recaptures the quality and significance of some past event or era via the expressions to which it gave rise. Such mental solidarity is an achievement made possible through a combination of empirical and imaginative work, and while understanding is always possible here it remains beyond our reach in the case of an historical actor, for instance, "to depict his or her life so precisely that the particular processes can be related in terms of cause and effect."[13] The reality of human freedom makes causal and predictive language impossible, but what is always possible for the human scientist is to relate particular to particular and both to a larger universality or context in a way that makes genuine understanding possible. We can and do understand the past – never perfectly, of course, but satisfactorily once we have done the often painstaking work of historical research. If we can never transport ourselves altogether into the past or into other minds, we can nonetheless understand the meaning of their expressions. Moreover, we can do so objectively, or such was the promise that Dilthey held out. Hermeneutics as he conceived it is an epistemological and objective enterprise, and while hermeneutical philosophers who followed in his wake would largely take a different view, for Dilthey research conducted in any of the human sciences is fully capable of reaching objective conclusions if it is properly conducted, or if we negotiate our way through the hermeneutic circle in a way that is empirically rigorous.

The term "historicism" in some (rather ambiguous) connotation has long been attached to Dilthey (among others, of course), and we must take a brief look at this phenomenon as well as the related issue of historical relativism. Objectivism and relativism are an odd couple, but both terms have been

---

[13] Ibid., 265.

associated with this thinker from the beginning. Historicism may be thought of in general terms as "a philosophy that emphasizes the importance of history in understanding, explaining, or evaluating phenomena," in the words of Mark Bevir.[14] On historian Geoffrey Barraclough's definition, historicism refers to a movement among nineteenth-century professional historians that sought to account for a given phenomenon through a close analysis of the chain of events that led up to it, and where "the underlying assumption [is] that the whole of reality is one vast historical process" and "the nature of everything which exists is comprehended in its historical development."[15] Such a developmental process is cumulative but not necessarily teleological, and no notion of progress is implied here. There is continuity in history, on the historicist view, but this ought not to be conceived as a secular counterpart to providence but something more organic in nature. Specialization and minutiae are important here, for the kind of detailed empirical work that historical research involves is what makes it possible to transpose oneself imaginatively into the past in the way that Dilthey and the historicists sought. Grasping specific relations – innumerable of them – between phenomena are what make historical and all human-scientific understanding possible.

In the nineteenth century the historical profession was anxious to establish its intellectual credentials in the university, and in a positivist era this meant giving it as scientific an appearance as possible. The "Historical School" endeavoured but, in his estimation, "failed – due to its lack of a truly empirical philosophy – to attain a knowledge of socio-historical reality which uses clear concepts and tenets," and it fell to Dilthey to conceptualize "unprejudiced empirical inquiry as distinct from empiricism." The kind of empirical inquiry for which historicists called would be charged by critics with both an excessive antiquarianism due to its insistence upon knowing the past on its own terms and for its own sake and also with pedantry for the kind of minutiae that such investigation required. The past in its entirety, not only the larger events and famous personages in which historians had traditionally taken interest but the more commonplace as well, needed to be understood if what we are in search of is some larger comprehension of the spirit of a given age. Under the influence of romanticism as well, many a nineteenth-century historian worked with an organic conception of historical growth which was believed to unify the myriad elements and happenings of an era. Seeing this required "sympathetic immersion in the

---

[14] Mark Bevir, "Historicism and the Human Sciences in Victorian Britain" in *Historicism and the Human Sciences in Victorian Britain*, ed. Mark Bevir (Cambridge: Cambridge University Press, 2017), 2.

[15] Geoffrey Barraclough, "Universal History" in H. P. R. Finberg, ed. *Approaches to History* (Toronto: University of Toronto Press, 1962), 109.

details of the historical process, a universal approach to history aiming to determine the value of a particular state of affairs solely from the context of its development." The historical school, he added, "considered spiritual life as historical through and through and approached social theory historically, seeking the explanations and rules of contemporary life in the study of the past. New ideas flowed from it through countless channels into all the particular disciplines."[16] This school's methodological basis needed to be rethought, Dilthey proposed, and an empirically minded hermeneutics seemed the most promising candidate.

Complicating this is the consideration, to which Dilthey also drew attention, that historical understanding does not stand at any radical distance from its object, and indeed to the contrary. The promise of objectivity notwithstanding, the historical interpreter is not the "knowing subject" of so much modern epistemology, and indeed the latter notion is a fiction. In an often-cited passage, Dilthey wrote,

> No real blood flows in the veins of the knowing subject constructed by Locke, Hume, and Kant, but rather the diluted extract of reason as a mere activity of thought. A historical as well as psychological approach to whole human beings led me to explain even knowledge and its concepts (such as the external world, time, substance, and cause) in terms of the manifold powers of a being that wills, feels, and thinks.[17]

We are historical beings through and through, in every facet of our being. This, in the view of his critics, raised the spectre of historical relativism: are historians, or human scientists in general, trapped within the very standpoint that they seek to know objectively, since on Dilthey's view historians do not stand at any radical distance from their object? Anything in the human world, not least human beings themselves, is what it has become through the larger historical process and nothing outside it, but what now becomes of historical knowledge and its promise of objectivity? Later hermeneuticists in the main will jettison objectivity, at least in a naive form, but Dilthey wished to retain this ideal of modern epistemology while fully acknowledging the historical embeddedness of the interpreter's own perspective. Objectivity remains possible if the historian is able to place oneself imaginatively in the standpoint of some past era by interpreting its expressions while employing the concepts of that time. No Cartesian bracketing of one's own point of view is necessary here, although twentieth-century hermeneuticists would largely follow Heidegger in being skeptical of the possibility of transposing oneself into alien horizons precisely for the reason that we are historical beings all the way down. "What a man is," as

---

[16] Dilthey, *Introduction to the Human Sciences*, 130, 48.   [17] Ibid., 50.

Dilthey had stated, "only his history can tell him."[18] Human scientists are unable simply to bootstrap their way out of their culture or time period, yet he holds onto the promise that if they find their way about the hermeneutic circle with sufficient care, they may achieve something resembling this. The key is to regard every human phenomenon as neither static nor isolated but as belonging to a larger process of historical development, for the truth about our object is in every case dynamic and historical. No elaborate superstructure is needed to understand historical events but an attention to evidence and procedure.

To speak of historical "explanation" and "causality" cannot mean, then, what they were long taken to mean under the influence of empiricism and positivism which is an accounting of the efficient causes that produced a given event in the past. Human events do not have causes in this sense but meanings which call for interpretation. If we wish to speak of the causes of World War II, as a *façon de parler* perhaps, this can only connote the multitude of factors – actions, happenings, conditions, persons, and reasons – that influenced or led to a series of events, but where influencing and leading are not causing in the sense of natural science. When we are speaking of events in the human world, interpreters and their objects are of the same substance, as it were, and this fact of our hermeneutic situation precludes the sort of objectivism which many modern philosophers and others have sought. If Dilthey remained optimistic about historical objectivity, his successors did not, and it is to this matter that I now turn.

The second hypothesis pertains to what Gadamer would later call the universality of hermeneutical reflection, and it begins on a note of skepticism. As he would state in *Truth and Method*,

> Dilthey himself has pointed out that we understand historically because we are ourselves historical beings. This is supposed to make things easier epistemologically. But does it? ... Is not the fact that consciousness is historically conditioned inevitably an insuperable barrier to its reaching perfect fulfillment in historical knowledge? Hegel could regard this barrier as overcome by virtue of history's being superseded by absolute knowledge. But if life is the inexhaustible, creative reality that Dilthey thinks it, then must not the constant alteration of historical context preclude any knowledge from attaining to objectivity?[19]

Gadamer was advancing a couple of claims here. The first concerns the conditions that would enable objectivity: an absolute foundation of the kind that Hegel sought would render this epistemological goal achievable, but the fact of

---

[18] Wilhelm Dilthey, *Gesammelte Schriften*, vol. 8 (Stuttgart, 1957), 226.
[19] Gadamer, *Truth and Method*, 224–225.

our hermeneutic embeddedness renders such objectivity and the larger quest for certainty with which it is bound up unattainable. Moreover, when we take seriously the proposition that "we understand historically because we are ourselves historical beings," we gain insight into the historical (or any) interpreter's involvement in that which they endeavour to know. The knower and the known do not belong to alien worlds, and temporal distance is not a gulf so wide as to preclude the meeting of minds that historical inquiry seeks. Interpretation, Gadamer maintained, belongs not only to the historian's task but to the ontological condition of human beings, or the search for understanding belongs in a fundamental way to our experience of the world in general. Let us have a closer look at this hypothesis, beginning with the issue of temporal distance.

Gadamer proffered what may strike us as a counterintuitive claim, which is that the historian's temporal distance from their object is not an obstacle that separates so much as it is a precondition of understanding and "the supportive ground of the course of events in which the present is rooted." It was, he added,

> the naive assumption of historicism . . . that we must transpose ourselves into the spirit of the age, think with its ideas and its thoughts, not with our own, and thus advance toward historical objectivity. In fact the important thing is to recognize temporal distance as a positive and productive condition enabling understanding. It is not a yawning abyss but is filled with the continuity of custom and tradition, in the light of which everything handed down presents itself to us.

Dilthey's and the historicist's idea of interpretation as a "psychic transposition" is dubious on the grounds that this transcends what is possible for human reason, and also the human past is a living past on the basis of which we understand anything at all.[20] Tradition and the past itself are not over and done with but prepare, or have always already prepared, the ground on which we stand. Dilthey had spoken of the person and their world as opposite but inseparable poles of human life, and Gadamer would take a similar view of the tensional unity of past and present. There is no intelligible present without a past that has come down to us and that makes whatever is understood by us possible.

We are hermeneutic, which is to say speaking, beings who negotiate our way through the world by means of an understanding that is itself an effect of history, language, and culture. I shall discuss this theme in more detail in Section 2, but first, let us consider Gadamer's view on what he called the universality of hermeneutical reflection. Understanding and "preunderstanding" belong in a fundamental, and indeed ontological, way to what we do and what we are. The historian is but one instance of an interpreter who strives to understand their

---

[20] Ibid., 297, 396.

object not from the non-perspective of omniscience but from some contingent point of view or within a finite hermeneutic situation. Before and as an enabling condition of all overt cognition is an understanding that is an effect of the past and that is operative in all our efforts to know the truth about things. Our thinking is invariably embedded within and, so to speak, preformed by a tradition and a language which are our historical inheritance, and all of it – from the most conservative to the most critical (itself not an opposition) – is steeped in the tradition that we wish to place into view.

Let us have a look at a couple of passages in which Gadamer expressed this basic position:

> it seems to me there can be no doubt that the great horizon of the past, out of which our culture and our present live, influences us in everything we want, hope for, or fear in the future. History is only present to us in light of our futurity. Here we have all learned from Heidegger, for he exhibited precisely the primacy of futurity for our possible recollection and retention, and for the whole of our history.

As well,

> there is no societal reality, with all its concrete forces, that does not bring itself to representation in a consciousness that is linguistically articulated. Reality does not happen "behind the back" of language; it happens rather behind the backs of those who live in the subjective opinion that they have understood "the world" (or can no longer understand it); that is, reality happens precisely *within* language.[21]

The major claims being advanced here are that (1) understanding in general – including historical understanding – is situated in time; (2) it is equally situated in language; and (3) understanding is not only what we do but what we "are." In the first two claims, Gadamer pointed out that as a matter of phenomenological fact, human beings are creatures of time and language in ways that tend to escape our notice. Temporality, as Husserl and Heidegger in particular had noted, belongs to our experience of the world in general. The present moment is not an experiential atom but is embedded in a basic structure of retention and protention which remains largely in the background of our awareness. We "are," as Heidegger would say, at once our past and our future in the sense that, phenomenologically speaking, the historical present is experienced not as an isolated now-point but as arising from the past and as having an orientation to the future. The human past, both one's own and that of an historical community,

---

[21] Hans-Georg Gadamer, "The Universality of the Hermeneutical Problem" and "On the Scope and Function of Hermeneutical Reflection," both in *Philosophical Hermeneutics*, ed. and trans. David E. Linge (Berkeley: University of California Press, 1977), 8–9, 35.

is never over and done with, but rather, as Heidegger expressed it, "Dasein [the human being] always is how and 'what' it already was. Whether explicitly or not, it *is* its past," whether this be a socially shared or a personal past. The past provides a context for present experience and conveys an understanding of its meaning. A present event may be perceived as a continuation, a departure, or in some way a response to what came before. The present moment is not merely what it is but, insofar as it is understood, how it has come to pass. It is a living past that weighs upon the present, and while not everything is remembered from the past, what is remembered lives on by setting the stage for what is now happening. This is expressed in Heidegger's concept of thrownness: human beings find ourselves thrown into a lifeworld and in the midst of relations and concerns that provide us with a fundamental orientation. One is neither frozen in time – an eternal present – nor separate and apart from one's world but is a being-in-the-world, a being-with-others, and a profoundly temporal and historical being. Our lifeworld affords us with possibilities of what we may become and which reflect what others have done. The past lives, then, in the sense that the human being "grows into a customary interpretation of itself and grows up on that interpretation." Equally important is the future, which is also to be understood in its living character. We think, act, and choose in a sense of projecting forward on the basis of possibilities recovered from the past. One is what one does, or what one is continually in process of becoming, and is not an altogether stable entity of some kind. Just as the past weighs upon the present, so does the future in the sense that the meaning of one's present action is inseparable from what one is trying to bring about at a later time. The human being always has an unfinished quality, a "constant being-ahead-of-itself," in the sense that one is continually projecting a future for oneself and in this sense "is" one's future: "Dasein *is always already its not-yet* as long as it is."[22]

Intelligible human experience in general is mediated and shaped by language, and in this sense language preforms thought. This is what Gadamer referred to as the linguisticality of consciousness: wherever there is understanding, it has been made possible, and it is also limited, by language. We understand a given phenomenon when we are able to speak or to give an account of it and not sooner. When we find the language that "fits" the object – where to fit does not mean to correspond but to reveal it as the thing that it is or as a bearer of meaning – it has in a sense become illuminated and so understood. Historical understanding is not an exception to this, as evidenced by the fact that historians must write about the human past and continue writing about it. No matter how many books we have on

---

[22] Martin Heidegger, *Being and Time*, trans. Joan Stambaugh (Albany: State University of New York Press, 2010), 19, 235. Throughout this Element, all italics in quoted material are in the original text.

the American Revolution or the fall of the Roman Empire, the work of interpretation is forever unfinished as there is always more to say or some novel analysis that regards the event in some new and interesting light.

The third and ontological claim that an understanding that is linguistically mediated and situated in historical tradition is not merely what we "do" but what we "are" is likely the most frequently criticized hypothesis that has been directed against philosophical hermeneutics since the publication of *Truth and Method* in 1960. Gadamer's skepticism regarding objectivity has appeared to his critics, beginning with Jürgen Habermas, as paving the way for a kind of traditionalism or conservatism in which it becomes effectively impossible to critique those elements of our language and tradition that give rise to false consciousness or ideology in a Marxian sense of the term. What happens when that in which all our thought is embedded becomes an oppressive force, as for Habermas and other critical theorists it more than occasionally does. What is needed, on this view, is an objective standpoint in the form of a critical theory of society which is capable of holding the language and tradition in which we stand at arm's length. The debate that ensued between Gadamer and Habermas is a long and complex story which would take us somewhat far afield, but in short the rejoinder that Gadamer and more recent hermeneutical philosophers have offered to this often-repeated charge retains a skeptical note regarding any conception of rationality that would enable the social critic, historian, or anyone else to transcend their hermeneutic situation and behold the world in the altogether unprejudiced manner that Habermas thought both possible and necessary. As Gadamer expressed it,

> in all understanding, whether we are expressly aware of it or not, the efficacy of history is at work .... This, precisely, is the power of history over finite human consciousness, namely that it prevails even where faith in method leads one to deny one's own historicity .... Consciousness of being affected by history is primarily consciousness of the hermeneutical *situation*. To acquire an awareness of a situation is, however, always a task of peculiar difficulty. The very idea of a situation means that we are not standing outside it and hence are unable to have any objective knowledge of it. We always find ourselves within a situation, and throwing light on it is a task that is never entirely finished. This is also true of the hermeneutic situation – i.e., the situation in which we find ourselves with regard to the tradition that we are trying to understand. The illumination of this situation – reflection on effective history – can never be completely achieved; yet the fact that it cannot be completed is due not to a deficiency in reflection but to the essence of the historical being that we are. *To be historically means that knowledge of oneself can never be complete.* All self-knowledge arises from what is historically pregiven.[23]

---

[23] Gadamer, *Truth and Method*, 300–301.

I pick up this set of themes in Section 2, beginning with Heidegger's analysis of our "being-in-the-world" before discussing further Gadamer's conceptions of understanding and historical belonging.

2 Historical Belonging

What are the meaning and basis of Gadamer's statement that "the efficacy of history is at work" in all efforts to understand not only the historical past but everything in our human world?[24] Anything at all that is intelligible to us is intelligible because of certain underlying conditions of possibility which are at once operative upon reflection and largely hidden from us. Something is "at work" behind our back, and what that is he refers to here as "the efficacy of history." History is already at work upon us prior to our efforts to get it into view. Gadamer appropriated this phenomenological hypothesis from Heidegger, and it is to this thinker that I now turn.

Heidegger's analysis of historicity and temporality in *Being and Time*, as he expressly stated, is based upon "the pioneering investigations of Dilthey. Today's present generation has not as yet made them its own," he would write in 1927.[25] What Dilthey had brought to our attention is the fundamental nature of our participation in "socio-historical life" and the central place of understanding in that participation. We are historical beings through and through, and our being so conditions not only our investigations into the past but everything about us. We "belong" to history – but to say this immediately raises questions which Heidegger set out to address in his masterful work of 1927. Heidegger ranks among the most noteworthy and undoubtedly most influential philosophers of the twentieth century, and not least on account of his analysis of the topic that now concerns us, which is the nature of what we may call historical belonging. What does it mean to belong to or to participate in history? This is not the trivial claim that human beings find ourselves in history as one might find oneself in a room, for the latter is a contingency in a way that historical belonging is not.

We begin with what Heidegger in *Being and Time* famously called our "being-in-the-world." The human being itself, or Dasein (there-being or existence), always finds itself rooted in what Husserl and other phenomenological thinkers were calling a *Lebensweld*, a lifeworld or world of lived experience, social relations and practical involvements, language and culture, which is given to us and which forms the background against which our particular thoughts and actions occur. This is the world that we are in direct contact with, and it is pre-reflective, pre-scientific, and pre-philosophical. We do not

---

[24] Ibid., 301. [25] Heidegger, *Being and Time*, 360.

stand back from our lifeworld as a scientist holds a physical object at arm's length but stand out in the midst of it, are always already participating in it, and are, we might say, "of" it and not merely within it. Consider as an example the relationship that obtains between thought and the language in which it occurs. Thinking, as Plato famously put it, is "the talking of the soul with itself," and is thus a linguistic act, and where language itself is not a tool that we take up after acquiring a purpose but is there from the beginning. We think not merely "with" language but "in" it, in the activity of saying or articulating something in the same gesture that renders an object of thought intelligible. Gadamer would speak of language as the universal medium in which understanding takes place, and something similar characterizes the relation between our lifeworld and ourselves. We are in it and also of it, implicated in it, and already in the midst of it, as is thought already an act of language. As thought is entangled in language, "Dasein is also entangled in a tradition which it more or less explicitly grasps," as Heidegger expressed it. Being-in-the-world is "a fundamental structure of Dasein" in the sense that our participation in language and culture is at the root of the kind of being that we are.[26] It makes less sense to say that culture, language, and history belong to us than that we belong to them.

The significance of the hyphenated expression "being-in-the-world" is that the existing individual and its lifeworld are "a *unified* phenomenon" or two elements of a single fabric, an idea that stands in opposition to modern philosophers from Descartes and Hobbes onward for whom the self or the knowing subject stands at some remove from its world. "It is not the case," in Heidegger's words,

> that human being "is," and then on top of that has a relation of being to the "world" which it sometimes takes upon itself. Dasein is never "initially" a sort of a being which is free from being-in, but which at times is in the mood to take up a "relation" to the world. This taking up of relations to the world is possible only *because*, as being-in-the-world, Dasein is as it is.

Our mode of existing is to be already in relationship with a world of culture, language, social relations, and practical involvements of many kinds, none of which holds us captive, but they do set the terms in which our lives are played out. We are "in" a lifeworld not as a cow is in a barn but as a musical note belongs within a larger composition and assumes whatever meaning it holds in relation to that in which it resounds and the instrument on which it is played. The act of knowing or understanding "is already together with its world" and "is grounded beforehand in already-being-alongside-the-world, which essentially constitutes the being of Dasein."[27] Consider the archaeologist who unearths

---

[26] Ibid., 20.   [27] Ibid., 53, 57, 61.

some artifact from another time period and culture; they do not begin to comprehend it until they see it as "together with its world" or as a particular within a larger universality. We account for it by locating it in relation to its time and place, understanding the role it plays in a lifeworld, for without this the thing itself is bereft of significance. A bare item in a chronicle is mute until the historian takes it up into an account in which that item plays some role in light of which it becomes intelligible. An historical object has the ontological status of a relatum, and the same can be said of Dasein itself: a relation, or a complex network of these, subsists beneath and unifies human beings and their lifeworld.

Dilthey had maintained that since historians themselves are historical beings, that there is a consubstantiality as it were between researchers and their objects, this makes it possible for them to perform the kind of imaginative transposition into the past that he held out as an ideal of objective interpretation. A kind of psychological empathy brings us into contact with the past along with the innumerable matters that the human sciences investigate, and this occurs by virtue of the interpreter's ontological homogeneity with their object. Heidegger and Gadamer would modify this view significantly, and in a way that would cease to regard historical interpretation as an offshoot of psychology. The key concept is "belonging" which, as Gadamer pointed out,

> Heidegger was the first to unfold in its full radicality: that we study history only insofar as we are ourselves "historical" means that the historicity of human Dasein in its expectancy and its forgetting is the condition of our being able to re-present the past. What first seemed simply a barrier, according to the traditional concept of science and method, or a subjective condition of access to historical knowledge, now becomes the center of a fundamental inquiry.[28]

To say that we belong to history, to a lifeworld or tradition, means that we already and invariably stand within it and are also of it; we do not originally inhabit some presocial location – a state of nature or Cartesian poêle – and enter into a world as we might enter a shopping mall but are as unified with it as a musical note within a larger composition. As an historical event is only "historical" (historically significant) on condition that it is (capable of being) taken up into an account and does not stand alone, so a human being inhabits or dwells in its time and place from the root. It is a fundamentally relational being, and historicity defines a crucial aspect of our entanglement in a world. "Being-in-the-world," as Heidegger expressed it, "is always already entangled" in historical tradition, and it is this that makes historical understanding possible.[29] Both the historian and their object (be it an artifact, event, text,

---

[28] Gadamer, *Truth and Method*, 252. [29] Heidegger, *Being and Time*, 175.

work of art, document, personage, or what have you), in Gadamer's words, "have the *mode of being of historicity*."[30]

What, then, is the meaning of historicity? Heideggerian hermeneutics in *Being and Time* and other works and Gadamer's philosophical hermeneutics have both been designated a "hermeneutics of historicity," so what is this? At the heart of it are the concepts of understanding and history, both of which carry an important ontological connotation – they crucially pertain to our mode of being and are at the heart of what it is to be human – and both of which must also be regarded in their complementarity. Understanding is not merely one type of cognition but underlies cognition in general and constitutes our most basic form of relationship with a world from which we do not stand apart. In the continual search for intelligibility, or as Heidegger put it, in "directing itself toward" some matter

> and in grasping something, Dasein does not first go outside of the inner sphere in which it is initially encapsulated, but, rather, in its primary kind of being, it is always already "outside" together with some being encountered in the world already discovered. Nor is any inner sphere abandoned when Dasein dwells together with a being to be known and determines its character.[31]

The mind in grasping some truth about the world, like the historian conducting research into a past event, does not transport itself from some original location (an inner citadel of consciousness, the present) to another that is foreign to it but is already alongside or "with" the latter, and in a deeper sense of "with" than the carving fork is with the turkey. The latter two objects are wholly external to each other, although they are often found together. The knower and the known are not like this but are related internally. The historian is "outside" the present in the sense that one is directed toward the past, attuned to it, constituted by it, or in a manner of speaking "is" the past.

What is this "is"? Dasein, for Heidegger, "*is* its past," and its future as well. Again, the key concept is belonging: one belongs to one's past, and one's future, and one's larger historical community and tradition. Each of these belongs to us or constitutes the sort of being that we are and does not merely pertain to us as so many accidental qualities. They define us, so to speak, in a way that other things that pertain to us do not. There is a deeper affinity or sameness of being that relates us to our human past than to any traits, information, or property that we may be said to possess. We do not *have* a past; we *are* it. The past fundamentally orients our present, forms a background context against which everything that is presently before us may be understood, and also establishes parameters within which it is experienced and known. Historicity, our having been already formed within and by our historical past and our anticipation of a future, and temporality

---

[30] Gadamer, *Truth and Method*, 252. [31] Heidegger, *Being and Time*, 62.

History and Hermeneutics 25

must be understood in a deeper and more ontological way than philosophers have long supposed, including philosophers of history. Heidegger would speak of the human being's participation within time and history in terms of what he called "thrownness" and "projection." We are thrown into the world in the sense that we are constantly oriented toward some future that we anticipate and toward which we are on the way. Our most basic experience of time is not of an object distant from us but as something (which is not a thing) in which we stand and which supplies our present with a fundamental orientation in which we are, as he put it, "*stretched along*" and which we do not experience as a "succession of sheer 'nows.'" Historicity and temporality are more like modes than objects of experience, as when we say "now that ... the doors slams; now that ... my book is missing, etc." "Now" and "then" are not objects of experience but a way in which experiences are had or lived: "now that" the sun is high I should cut the lawn; "and then" there were three members of a rock band that had formerly had four, and five before that. Time is experienced in this manner, as pulling us along incessantly toward what is next. We do not, then, become temporal or enter time from some place outside it, as may be said equally of history. As Heidegger asked, "Is Dasein factically already "objectively present" beforehand, and then at times gets into 'a history'? Does Dasein first *become* historical through a concatenation of circumstances and events? Or is the being of Dasein first constituted by occurrence, so that *only because Dasein is historical in its being* are anything like circumstances, events, and destinies ontologically possible?"[32] We are historical and temporal in our being, and it is because of this that we are able to become responsible for what is passed down to us by tradition.

Temporality is not an incidental feature of human experience but belongs to it in a fundamental way. Human experience has what phenomenologists following Husserl call a retentional-protentional structure: our experience of the present moment is not of something that simply is but of something that has come about, as memories of what has been supplying whatever is now happening with an intelligibility which makes it possible to cope with the present. The past is held onto and is a living past in the sense that it orients us in particular ways and prepares us for what is now happening, while protentions or anticipations prepare us for what is to come. Our experience "stretches along" and transcends the now in looking both forward – expecting, dreading, planning – and backward – remembering and holding onto experiences in light of which what is now happening makes sense. Human experience is encompassing in this way, as is illustrated in the case of listening to a piece of music. Our most basic experience here is not one of now X, now Y, now Z, where X, Y, and Z are heard in isolation

---

[32] Ibid., 19, 390, 389, 362.

but instead form a continuous flow of rhythm, leading, building and releasing tension, refraining, and in various ways relating one moment or element to another. In the experience of conversation, similarly one hears what another has to say in light of what they have already said or the question that prompted their response while also anticipating the direction the conversation is taking. All human experience is like this, while the bare now is an abstraction from experience as it is actually had by us.

Time as Heidegger described it is not what we might call clock-time and indeed is not a noun so much as an adverb: we do not perceive time as we would a pencil, but we experience what is before us as happening temporally. His concern was not to answer Augustine's question regarding the nature of time itself but to describe phenomenologically what it is or means to exist temporally. How does time appear to us if not as a thingly being? In going about answering this, he would draw an important distinction between our "primordial" or "authentic" way of experiencing time and its inauthentic mode. In the latter, we experience time as a mere succession of "nows" which come from nothing and lead to nothing, with each moment resembling a photograph that arrests the flow of events. Here, there is no before and after, no recollection or expectation, and no trajectory by which to understand how things are tending or to what they may be leading. There is no story here but a chronicle-like experience in which meaning eludes us. Authentic temporality is unlike this in that "the 'flux' of nows" is replaced with an experience that is pulled along by the course of events.[33] The present moment is experienced as having been prepared, set up, led up to, or haunted by a past that is itself a living heritage. Our habitual thoughts and actions have set the stage for what is now happening, and it is this temporal context that makes it possible to grasp what is taking place. The same is true of futurity: we "are" the future as well in the sense that the now is directed toward some projected future. It is pregnant with possibilities, a means to an end, part of a project, or it portends trouble. Such possibilities belong to our "primordial" or most basic experience of the present and are not imposed upon it from outside, as may be said of our heritage. This too belongs to us and to every intelligible experience. The tensed nature of our language reflects the basic fact of our experience that what is happening now is not simply what is but what has resulted or come about, is becoming or repeating, and will have been. A temporality-less existence – one that is wholly without retention and protention, memory and aims, anticipations and possibilities – would be a disorienting flux where everything appears from out of the blue and disappears into nothingness. Authentic historicity and

---

[33] Ibid., 401.

temporality likewise are a participation in a course of events that precedes and will also succeed us. This larger course is not an artificial imposition but belongs to our experience as it is lived. It is already pre-organized or pre-figured by a temporal structure that is inseparable from the kind of being that we are.

Our belonging within time and history is closely associated with our participation in language. Philosophical hermeneutics here advances a few claims that are bound up together: historical, and all, understanding is situated in both time and language, while understanding itself possesses ontological, not merely psychological or epistemological, import. Intelligible human experience is temporally and also linguistically embedded, such that there is a primordial belonging together of past, present, and future, of the interpreter and their object, and also of language and object, while each of these basic facts of our experience remains elusive to our comprehension. How is it possible that anything in our experience is intelligible at all? This is surely one of the most central questions of philosophy, and it goes to the heart as well of what Gadamer called "the hermeneutical phenomenon." Much and perhaps all that appears self-evident to us has been made possible by a rich heritage of history and culture at the heart of which is the language in which experiences are had by us. Understanding itself is a "coming into language of what has been said in the tradition: an event that is at once appropriation and interpretation."[34] To understand a past event or any human phenomenon is to interpret (to see-as, read, characterize, classify, disclose) it with respect to its meaning and so to appropriate it or to bring it within one's conceptual and linguistic world. It is to speak of it as the thing that it is or as bearing significance, value, or truth.

In the case of historical interpretation, under what conditions is an event, artifact, or personage designated as "historical"? That it belongs to the past is insufficient here. What colour of tie John F. Kennedy was wearing when he was assassinated is not historically significant on the basis that it is irrelevant to and does not advance the *histoire*; it sheds no light upon and bears no relation to the events of that day – and if somehow an historian were to discover such a relation, it would take on historical significance at that time and on that condition. It must be capable of being absorbed within an account – which is likely to be a narrative – and not stand alone as Kennedy's tie appears to do. We are interested in "what happened," but not everything that happened but what bears a meaning that is borne along by the account. The price of beer in Dallas on that day similarly is not historical, unless it factors in some other account unrelated to the assassination. An historical account is a linguistic act; we are recounting what took place and how it may be understood. As Gadamer stated,

---

[34] Gadamer, *Truth and Method*, 404, 459.

"historical understanding proves to be a kind of literary criticism writ large" for the reason that where literary interpretation takes a particular text as its object, historical interpretation takes into view the tradition in a larger sense. Interpretation is one and the same even as its object changes or becomes relatively general or specific. Language is there from the beginning and "is a medium where I and world meet or, rather, manifest their original belonging together." Speaking generally, our "relation to the world is absolutely and fundamentally verbal in nature, and hence intelligible. Thus hermeneutics is ... a *universal aspect of philosophy*, and not just the methodological basis of the so-called human sciences."[35] It is a universal aspect of history no less, since the same belonging together of intelligibility and language is found here as well.

We may think of the historian, or indeed all of us who seek to understand our world, as a mediator of a kind. One stands always in the middle, not in some location that is altogether external to that which we are endeavouring to know but in between language and object, present and past, or in a standpoint that encompasses both. The present historical moment, like language itself, is not something in which we are ever entrapped but a horizon that remains on the move, open to what more may be said and experienced. Gadamer invoked the metaphor of the horizon to describe the nature of historical consciousness and to bring to light the error that he saw within Dilthey's account. The latter, to recall, held out an ideal of historical interpretation as a transposition, at once imaginative and objective, into the past, essentially a leaving behind of the present in order to enter a foreign world. As so many have said, we must understand the past on its own terms and not simply subsume it within categories of our present era and culture. Hermeneuticists also maintain this, but with a difference. "Are there really," as Gadamer asked, "two different horizons here – the horizon in which the person seeking to understand lives and the historical horizon within which he places himself? Is it a correct description of the art of historical understanding to say that we learn to transpose ourselves into alien horizons?"[36] His negative answer stems from the consideration that a horizon – understood as everything that may be experienced from a particular vantage point and the limits of that vantage point – is neither closed nor frozen in time but is continually on the move with us and open to further interrogation. We should not conceive of the present and the past as two closed circles between which is a divide which the historian must somehow venture across, for these circles are never closed but open onto a world that is encompassing. Think of one's own personal history here: when we recall some episode from our past, we are neither bridging a divide nor leaving the present behind but tracing relations between then and now and, as it were,

---

[35] Ibid., 335, 469, 471.   [36] Ibid., 303.

conversing with a past that remains living. We "are" our past – also our present and our future – and accordingly when we bring some element of the past to light we are not travelling through time but participating in a dialectic or a dialogue of a kind.

For Gadamer, Hegel was correct in his view that the historian is engaged "not in the restoration of the past but in *thoughtful mediation with contemporary life*. Hegel is right when he does not conceive of such thoughtful mediation as an external relationship established after the fact but places it on the same level as the truth of art itself."[37] The historian mediates between past and present as the art critic mediates between a work of art's truth claim and an audience. Gadamer's aesthetics is a rather long and complex story, but at the heart of it is his view that the work of art issues a claim to truth and does not merely please, entertain, or otherwise appeal to the affects. There is truth in art, as Heidegger also maintained, where truth connotes not a correspondence between statements and facts but an opening up or revealing (*aletheia*) of some meaningful dimension of the phenomena. Art neither argues nor hypothesizes but shows, takes something that had been shrouded in mystery and "unconceals" it as the thing that it is or as bearing some meaning which is there for us to experience and engage with. Aesthetic experience is not an "external relationship" between artwork and audience where the latter seeks a "restoration" of the artist's intention but a fundamentally different sort of encounter where we are listening to and potentially being transformed by a truth claim. Art speaks, and what it has to say calls for the thoughtful interpretation and response of an audience again on the model of a dialectic where we may speak of the interpreter and the work itself as participating in a process that encompasses them both. The professional critic does not stand outside this process but as a mediator within it, as a relatively experienced interpreter who is able to shed light without playing the expert. The relationship between audience, critic, and the work itself is invariably "internal" in the sense that all are engaged in a process of seeking intelligibility within a given medium of expression.

Of course, there is far more to Gadamer's aesthetics than this, but for our purposes this will suffice to clarify the analogy just alluded to between aesthetic and historical consciousness. Both involve a kind of mediation where the interpreter pursues the truth while seeking what he called a "fusion of horizons" between that of the interpreter and their object. "*Understanding*" in general, whether its object is a work of art, text, past event, or anything else in our world, "*is to be thought of less as a subjective act than as participating in an event of tradition*, a process of transmission in which past and present are constantly

---

[37] Ibid., 161.

mediated." In the case of the historical past, we are not transcending our own ostensibly closed standpoint and entering a different (also closed) one but "rising to a higher universality" which includes the horizon of the past together with the present in a kind of tensional unity. Gadamer clarified his position this way:

> When our historical consciousness transposes itself into historical horizons, this does not entail passing into alien worlds unconnected in any way with our own; instead, they together constitute the one great horizon that moves from within and that, beyond the frontiers of the present, embraces the historical depths of our self-consciousness. Everything contained in historical consciousness is in fact embraced by a single historical horizon. Our own past and that other past toward which our historical consciousness is directed help to shape this moving horizon out of which human life always lives and which determines it as heritage and tradition.[38]

It is a valid goal of historical research to understand the past on its own terms rather than simply file it within familiar pigeonholes, but we often mistake this understanding something – whether a past event, artwork, text, conversation partner, or whatever it is – "on its own terms" again as leaping beyond the supposedly closed circle of the present and into the closed circle of the past where no such act is possible or even necessary. The two horizons open onto each other, just as two speakers of a language may enter into a conversation without exiting any inner sphere. So does the historian stand to the past, not as a time traveller to a distant world but as an interlocutor in a world that includes them both. The model of ordinary conversation is apt here, where interlocutors are attempting not to enter each other's heads or re-experience their experience but to understand in common the truth about some matter and so to achieve a meeting of minds. No transposing into the alien is involved here but an opening onto another who is never altogether foreign.

Such mediation with the past is less a "constructing" than a listening. I shall return to the concept of construction later, but historical consciousness is not a one-way reading into or imposition upon the past of the historian's point of view but a far more receptive listening to a past that continues to speak to us. There is truth in history, and in a sense that must be clarified. To speak of historical truth here connotes something additional to the consideration that the human past contains facts – names, dates, facts, and figures – which the historian must "get right." They must indeed, but something more is involved than this, for the chronicle also gets the facts right without achieving historical understanding in a richer sense. An account of the past speaks to us in a way that

---

[38] Ibid., 291, 304, 303.

History and Hermeneutics 31

a chronicle does not; it strives for a truth that is less a simple enumeration of facts than an allowing for the past or something within it to speak to us. An encounter with the past involves a fusion of horizons where past and present are brought into a dialogue that allows something to emerge and "is not merely a reproductive but always a productive activity as well." We are "producing" a truth not in a constructivist sense, which is closer to an imposition than the kind of production of which Gadamer was speaking, but as an artistic performance is a production that seeks not to re-present some original state (such as what the artist had in mind or the first presentation of a work) but something that is in some measure new and different. He would also generalize the point: "we understand in a *different* way, *if we understand at all*."[39] We do not understand the past better than our predecessors, including those contemporary to the period we are researching, but differently and in light of our ongoing operations within the hermeneutic circle.

What is truth in history but an interpretive disclosure that allows the past to speak to us from and about itself but that also speaks to a contemporary audience in some measure differently from how it has spoken in the past. We do not, by the nature of human understanding itself, comprehend the Protestant Reformation in quite the way that our predecessors did either in the sixteenth century or at any intervening time due to the ongoing effects, appropriations, and reactions that continue to issue from it. The names and dates are what they are, but the story has been told and retold and will continue to be because of its ongoing relationship with a present that is always on the move. If there will be human beings in this world in a thousand years, they will understand the Reformation differently than we do, while we ourselves are far from regarding this phenomenon in a single light. To distinct audiences, any historical phenomenon shows itself differently. It may be helpful here to draw a distinction between historical facts and historical truth. What exactly is a fact is a difficult philosophical question, as of course is the case with truth. The more general issue may be left to one side so that we may focus for a moment upon the specific question of the relation between an historical fact and historical truth. It is an historical fact that on the 31st of October, 1517, one Martin Luther published his *Ninety-five Theses*. It is an historical truth that this event sparked a movement the consequences of which remain with us. The first was fully known on the date of its occurrence, but its meaning was not. Its meaning on the day itself was contingent upon its then-future consequences, and understanding this requires retrospection. Truth here is a function of an event's meaning or meanings as they develop over time and is partial, aspectival, and contingent without being a matter of pure invention on the historian's part. Historical truth

---

[39] Ibid., 296.

does not drift far from the shore of facts, but it does show itself differently at different times and to different interpreters depending upon ongoing relations between the facts themselves and everything that is consequent upon them. Future historians will not cease to write about the Reformation not only because not all the facts are currently known but more importantly because the event itself and the facts that it encompasses are likely to be regarded in a light that we cannot currently anticipate and related to other considerations than to date have happened or drawn our attention. Facts themselves may be thought of as unnegotiable touchstones which, once empirically established, any historical account making a legitimate claim to truth must incorporate but which also underdetermine the account itself. A good chronicle might set down all the facts (although this is disputable if relevance is itself a function of interpretation), but what it could not do is reveal in full their capacity to disclose meaning. What happened on October 31, 1517 is an uncontestable fact which from the perspective of our own time and concepts shows itself under an aspect that is true without being totalizing or closing off the possibility of further interpretation.

As Gadamer stated, "To think historically always involves mediating between those ideas [of the past] and one's own thinking. To try to escape from one's own concepts in interpretation is not only impossible but manifestly absurd. To interpret means precisely to bring one's own preconceptions into play so that the text's meaning can really be made to speak for us." We are not forced to choose between, on one hand, a thoroughgoing objectivism where historical facts are fully determinate in their being and speak for themselves and, on the other, a relativism for which historical truth is relative either to the perspective of the interpreter, a time period, or anything else. Gadamer and more recent hermeneutical philosophers regard this as a false dichotomy and defend an intermediate view which continues to speak of truth, facts, and evidence without making an idol of such concepts. Historians are no more able to place their perspective on a shelf than philosophers are, but it does not follow that they are incapable of genuinely listening to the past. The fusion of horizons of which Gadamer spoke "is not a mysterious communion of souls, but sharing in a common meaning," and where sharing involves a constant back-and-forth movement between asking questions and listening for a response that might surprise us.[40] As one contemporary philosopher puts it, the hermeneuticist must

> do battle simultaneously on two fronts: against, on the one hand, the object-
> ivism of Romantic hermeneutics (and traditional metaphysics more gener-
> ally) and, on the other hand, the relativism extolled by a number of
> postmodernists (who assert that since no single interpretation of a text or

---

[40] Ibid., 398, 292.

anything else can – as hermeneutics itself maintains – legitimately claimed to be the one and only correct or valid interpretation, a state of glorious, freewheeling interpretational anarchy must necessarily prevail).[41]

Let us try to clarify further Gadamer's claim mentioned previously that historical understanding essentially involves a mediation between the past and the historian's own thinking about it. What is being mediated and what is the nature of such mediation? To the first question, what we have spoken of as a living past is appropriately conceived not in the manner of a substance that is determinate and wholly unchanging but as a relatum. Historical facts themselves are determinate and unchanging, but what is neither is the mode in which they become intelligible for us, their meaning or indeed their truth. The facts themselves are mute apart from the language by which the historian brings them to light or the role they play in an interpretive account; they do not speak but are spoken for by the historian, and phenomenologically we cannot separate the historical object from the manner of its coming to be understood. The past is comprehensible in relation to the present and from the point of view of the historian who stands within it. To historical consciousness belongs the task of opening itself to what speaks to us in tradition, while tradition itself, as Paul Ricoeur expressed it, is "not the inert transmission of some already dead deposit of material but the living transmission of an innovation."[42] The past is indeed "other" than the present, and while it can still be said that we strive to understand the past "as it really was" and "on its own terms," "as it was" cannot be disentangled from how it appears from our present standpoint and "its own terms" are only visible through the medium of our own. The horizons of the past we are endeavouring to understand and the present from which alone understanding is possible are fused or brought into a dialogue which does not culminate in any final account.

The second question concerns the sense in which historians mediate these two horizons, and the model is a conversation between a past that addresses us and an historian who listens openly while also questioning, anticipating, and configuring what they hear. This sense of mediation is neither wholly passive – receiving as a blank slate what is inscribed on it externally – nor wholly active – legislating all that comes before it – but is attuned to what speaks to us from the past as an interlocutor or a text. Gadamer articulated the point as follows:

> Of course the reader before whose eyes the great book of world history simply lies open does not exist. But neither does the reader exist who,

---

[41] Gary Madison, "On the Importance of Getting Things Straight" in *Hermeneutic Philosophies of Social* Science, ed. Babette Babich (Berlin: de Gruyter, 2019), 192.

[42] Paul Ricoeur, *Time and Narrative* vol. 1, trans. Kathleen McLaughlin and David Pellauer (Chicago: University of Chicago Press, 1990), 68.

when he has his text before him, simply reads what is there. Rather, all reading involves application, so that a person reading a text is himself part of the meaning he apprehends. He belongs to the text that he is reading.[43]

Again, the operative term is "belonging": the historian belongs to history, has always already been constituted by it, but also listens to it as a partner in conversation listens to another in a relationship that is reciprocal. The "application" that all interpretation involves refers to the fact that in all reading and listening, from the most receptive to the most critical, interpreters inevitably bring their own conceptual framework with them and apply it to an object. Whatever truth emerges is the product of a joint undertaking, a sharing and a participating in a past that continues to speak to us and to which we reply as partners in a dialogue that is perpetual. Interpreters bring with them an inheritance of tradition and pre-reflective judgments – what Gadamer called "prejudices" – which for the most part operate behind our backs and which are both inescapable and indispensable in all understanding. When an historian, for instance, initially encounters a document, he or she projects or anticipates a meaning of the document as a whole on the basis of a preliminary glance where perhaps the document's title or the opening words suggest a significance for the whole. The reader anticipates what is to come, and the course of the reading confirms or disconfirms this initial prejudice. The central business of interpretation involves sorting out which of our anticipations are true, in the sense that they shed light on the text as a whole, and which are false or lead to incoherence and contradiction between one passage and another. Prejudices may be true or false, but there is no eliminating them from the course of interpretation since meaning only emerges as a response to a question the interpreter has posed and through the confirmation or disconfirmation of our anticipations. In finding our way about the hermeneutic circle, we are looking back and forth from the meaning of a particular word, phrase, or passage to the meaning of the text as a whole and vice versa, and continually revising our understanding in light of what emerges in this dialectical process. It remains an important task of historical inquiry to become aware of our prejudices to the extent that this is possible, but there are limits here, as it is an undertaking that may be compared to examining the poles of a raft that is sustaining us. "It is," as the same philosopher put it, "the tyranny of hidden prejudices that makes us deaf to what speaks to us in tradition."[44] Not prejudices in general but false and especially hidden ones block the course of intellectual inquiry while true prejudices are confirmed by rendering our object of knowledge coherent.

---

[43] Gadamer, *Truth and Method*, 335.   [44] Ibid., 272.

To say that "the efficacy of history is at work" in historical and all human understanding means that we investigate the past neither as an empiricist's *tabula rasa* nor on the basis of a rationalist's clear and distinct ideas alone but as a sharer in a heritage that tradition has already afforded us. In all such investigations, the historian strives to become open to the past as it shows itself, without imagining that our openness is either unlimited, unconditioned, or uncritical. However critical or convention-defying our interpretation of the past becomes, it remains one form of our participation in history rather than a knowledge that wholly transcends it. This form of knowledge culminates in what we may speak of a "sense of history" which includes while surpassing the factual information that the historian gathers. To cite Gadamer once more, "whoever has a historical sense knows what is possible for an age and what is not, and has a sense of the otherness of the past in relation to the present." As is true of a musical sense, a historical sense is a broad and affectively charged understanding of a certain domain of meaning and is more open, discerning, and conscientious toward its object than the mind that merely possesses information. There is an "immediacy" about a sense which "knows how to make sure distinctions and evaluations in the individual case without being able to give its reasons."[45] The reasons are more likely to be felt than known in a sense of being directly statable and justifiable conclusions from an argument or evidence. Historical research involves no little reasoning and is rigorous and poetic in about equal measure. The more poetic dimension of this is the theme to which I now turn.

3 Narrative Configuration and Prefiguration

Dilthey believed that "The human mind has a peculiar need to narrate deeds and to hear them narrated," and it is a need that factors deeply into what historians do.[46] Historians are storytellers; it is right there in the Latin word "*historia*" and is not difficult to see when we read the often lengthy accounts of the rise and fall of empires, the careers of historical personages, wars, and so on. Such accounts typically if not always have a beginning, a middle, and an end, and if the narrative structure is not always easy to identify, it does tend to be at least implicit in the accounts that historians craft for their readers. It aims, of course, to be a "true story" rather than a fictional one, or if it begins to drift too far from the shore of historical fact then we tend to designate it by another name – historical fiction, fictional history, or some such term. The problem is that "stories" and most everything that pertains to them – art, poetry, literature, fiction, metaphor, imagination – fit rather awkwardly into a modern worldview that has a decided

---

[45] Ibid., 15. [46] Dilthey, *Hermeneutics and the Study of History*, 261.

preference for such weighty matters as truth, facts, evidence, proof, explanation, causality, and similar concepts which comprise a worldview that is at least implicitly metaphysically materialist and epistemologically empiricist. In a time when science and technology exercise such a thorough hold on culture, narrative has a tendency to be regarded as intellectually unserious in comparison with the values just mentioned. Many an historian has aspired to leave it out of their work altogether, from the positivists of Dilthey's era to the more recent Annales school. Yet it remains that narrative at least appears to be what Barbara Hardy has called "a primary act of mind transferred to art from life" rather than (optionally) transferred to historical life from art.[47] Narrative appears stubbornly ineliminable not only from historical understanding but from understanding in general, a weed in the positivist's garden which if uprooted would effectively uproot the plants that are proximal to it.

When confronted with so unwelcome a visitor, the gardener is well advised to leave the weed where it is or perhaps to cut it off at ground level, even knowing that it is sure to grow back upon the next rain. If its roots may not be disentangled from the plants one values, it is best to make one's peace with it, and this may well be the predicament of the hard-nosed empiricist when confronted with the narrative form. Such a view began to emerge in the 1960s in the writings of philosophers of history such as W. B. Gallie, Arthur Danto, and Morton White, who were soon followed by Louis Mink, Hayden White, F. R. Ankersmit, and hermeneutical philosopher Paul Ricoeur, most especially in the latter's three-volume *Time and Narrative*. The principal objection to the view that each of them was espousing (with notable variations, of course) is that history as a discipline strives to be empirical, objective, and perhaps scientific while the accent these writers were placing on the storyteller's art overemphasizes the aesthetic and so detracts from the claim to scientificity. Since then, a central debate among philosophers of history and many historians themselves has concerned the self-image of this field of knowledge and whether it is more suitably aligned with science, literature, or something else such as politics. The "narrativists," as they have been called, have sometimes aligned themselves with hermeneutics but far more so with the poststructuralism and postmodernism which have exercised such dramatic influence across the disciplines from the 1960s through the present day. Undoubtedly the most influential theorist in this field from the previously mentioned list has been Hayden White whose *Metahistory* of 1973 accentuates the literary, aesthetic, and also ethical-political dimensions of historical writing far more than the empirical and scientific.

---

[47] Barbara Hardy, "Towards a Poetics of Fiction: An Approach through Narrative," *Novel: A Forum on Fiction* 2, no. 1 (Autumn 1968), 5.

What, in broad terms, has been the case for narrative as a central phenomenon within historical inquiry? On the face of it, this hypothesis has faced an uphill climb, and for two main reasons. The first is general: in a scientific age it is something of an imperative in nearly all disciplines to play up the empirical and methodological dimensions of the field for the simple purpose of achieving intellectual respectability. The second reason is more specific to history: it is indisputable that historians spend a great deal of their time sifting through evidence in about as empirically rigorous a manner as any of the social sciences and, more arguably, the natural sciences as well. They are certainly not making it up, as has been said of storytellers from ancient times. Poets in particular, as Plato gave us some reason to believe, lie, and not just occasionally. Historians, by contrast, are neither liars, novelists, nor fantasists but empirically minded compilers of evidence about what actually happened in the past. There is a certain common-sense empiricism at work here: the work of the historian is to gather together and to evaluate tremendous quantities of evidence, facts, statistics, documents, names and dates, and so on, and in the end to assemble it all in an account that reports the truth about what took place. Dressing it up into an aesthetically pleasing form is not the professional historian's task – the popular historian's task perhaps, but not the more serious task of the academic. What has been the narrativists' reply? The replies have been several and do not necessarily call for a rejection of common-sense empiricism. Let us hear briefly from a couple of representative theorists, beginning with Hayden White:

> There is ... a certain necessity in the relationship between the narrative, conceived as a symbolic or symbolizing discursive structure, and the representation of specifically historical events. This necessity arises from the fact that human events are or were products of human actions, and these actions have produced consequences that have the structures of texts – more specifically, the structure of narrative texts. The understanding of these texts, considered as the product of actions, depends upon our being able to reproduce the processes by which they were produced, that is, to narrativize these actions. Since these actions are in effect lived narrativizations, it follows that the only way to represent them is by narrative itself.[48]

Hermeneutical philosopher Richard Kearney puts it this way: "History-telling is never literal .... It is always at least in part *figurative* to the extent that it involves telling according to a certain selection, sequencing, emplotment and perspective. But it does try to be *truthful*."[49]

---

[48] Hayden White, *The Content of the Form: Narrative Discourse and Historical Representation* (Baltimore: Johns Hopkins University Press, 1987), 54.
[49] Richard Kearney, *On Stories* (London: Routledge, 2001), 136.

Kearney's last point is rather important: to say that historians are storytellers is not to echo Plato's view regarding the poets – that, however beautiful their works, they are a few steps removed from reality and have an unfortunate propensity for lying – but to draw attention to the artful dimension of historical inquiry. They indeed seek, and more than occasionally find, what we may continue to call the truth, but it is not the nature of historical truth to stand aloof from the selection of credible and relevant evidence, placing such matters into the correct sequence, arranging a plot that holds the facts together in some intelligible order, and presenting the whole from a certain perspective. To advance the claim that a work of history is "at least in part *figurative*" is not to say that it is unempirical, "subjective" (if this means that it sheds more light upon the historian than history), or fanciful. Common-sense empiricism remains, but it also underdetermines the work of historical inquiry and the texts in which it culminates. A work of history typically if not always not only has a beginning, middle, and end structure but exhibits a good many other devices that we are not incorrect to call "literary," from themes and repetition to metaphor, allegory, synecdoche, foreshadowing, irony, tragedy, hyperbole, cliché, cautionary tales, and an entire tropology that is at the historian's disposal and often enough working behind their back, including when they would prefer to foreswear such niceties and get on with the business of relating what really happened. The narrativist's position is that "what really happened" and the story in which it is related are as inseparable as facts and truth, content and form, the message and the medium.

White's point concerns what he saw as a necessary relationship between narrative and the events and actions that comprise human history. An historian's account of an event

> remains something less than a proper history if he has failed to give to reality the form of a story. Where there is no narrative, Croce said, there is no history. And Peter Gay, writing from a perspective directly opposed to the relativism of Croce, puts it just as starkly: "Historical narration without analysis is trivial, historical analysis without narration is incomplete." Gay's formulation calls up the Kantian bias of the demand for narration in historical representation, for it suggests, to paraphrase Kant, that historical narratives without analysis are empty, while historical analyses without narrative are blind .... [H]istorical events dispose themselves to the percipient eye as stories waiting to be told, waiting to be narrated.[50]

The necessity in the relationship between narrative and human events lies in the nature of the events themselves, which are actions, situations, and decisions which must be understood in the way that such phenomena give themselves to

---

[50] White, *The Content of the Form*, 5–6.

be understood. Here matters become somewhat more complex, for a difficult question we shall need to confront is whether we may speak at all of human events "giving themselves" to us or whether it is the historian who determines as an autonomous literary choice how to "represent" such events. Is there any sense in which, as we often say of fictional narratives, stories "tell themselves" or is the interpreter wholly free to craft a story in a way of their choosing? In White's view narrative is a device of the literary imagination that imposes significance upon human events by arranging them into some meaningful order and genre, either tragedy, comedy, satire, or romance. The selection of a genre is essentially an aesthetic and moral choice that belongs to the historian and in no way belongs to the events themselves.

The hermeneutical philosopher sees this differently, and it begins with the concepts of temporality, historicity, and historical belonging. Historians, on this view, are tasked with understanding the past "as it really was" and "on its own terms," and where this is ultimately inseparable from how it appears from our perspective and through the medium of our own time, culture, and language. Historians belong to history in a fundamental, ontological sense of the word, and our mode of belonging conditions how past events will become intelligible for us. There is always a "for us" quality to interpretation, yet where this does not shade into an interpretive subjectivism, relativism, or constructivism. It is the events themselves – "the things themselves," in Husserl's phrase – that are the objects of understanding, and where there is no basis for positing a dichotomy between appearance and reality. When historians succeed in their task, the past shows itself to us, speaks to us, yet it speaks not for itself but through Hermes-like mediators whose business is to bring about a fusion of horizons between past and present. The meaningful dimension of a given event comes to light for us and is not imposed by the historian. Narrative is a mode of interpretation that is constantly employed in the human sciences whether researchers themselves are explicitly aware of it or (probably more often) not, whether we are speaking of historians, sociologists, anthropologists, economists, or what have you. Philosophers too are storytellers of a kind, albeit usually below the surface. This broader proposition need not concern us here, but what does is the hermeneutical hypothesis that historical understanding takes narrative form, and where the story itself is not a one-way bestowal of meaning but a dialogue with the past.

Why should we speak of a dialogue with the past, and what sort of dialogue is this? The concept of dialogue calls to mind two or more interlocutors who speak each for themselves and who by turns pose and respond to questions in a shared search for understanding about some subject matter. The past, or the kind of happenings that historians commonly concern themselves with, does not speak in this sense. Does it speak at all, or are we being fanciful here? Indeed, it does speak to us, but much depends on how we understand this. Does a document, for instance, speak? It does in the minimal sense that it contains words and perhaps sentences, but to the historian falls the task of making it speak in a larger sense. Does a battle or war speak? Again, it does in a preliminary way: presidents, generals, and so on do utter any number of statements about military goals and what not, but here too the historian must discern the significance of this event in a broader sense and with the benefit of a retrospection that is never available to the actors themselves. We do not understand the fall of the Roman Empire in quite the way that the Romans did. Instead, we configure – and must configure by the nature of historical understanding – what took place, and in doing so we do not bestow meaning onto events but allow this to emerge as we attend to the events themselves, on the model of listening to a partner in conversation. If historians are in a manner of speaking listeners, to what are they listening? Ricoeur suggested that it is "our confused, unformed, and at the limit mute temporal experience" to which the historian attends, while the art of interpretive listening itself is a reconfiguring of that experience into something that is less confused or mute. The historian brings that experience of the past into language and so renders it intelligible. "I see in the plots we invent," he added, "the privileged means by which we re-configure" that experience.[51] What did he mean by this?

Ricoeur and Gadamer are widely regarded as the foremost representatives of phenomenological or philosophical hermeneutics after Heidegger, so let us spend some time examining Ricoeur's contribution to the philosophy of history. The heart of his account bears upon the nature of historical understanding as taking an explicitly narrative form, although he would conceive this in a different light than White and numerous other defenders of narrative history. The historian's task is to fashion an account of a given set of events which contains a beginning, middle, and end structure and which manages to integrate into a unity the disparate actors, actions, intentions, consequences, circumstances, random happenings, causes and laws (if any there be), and anything else that is relevant to the events we are bringing to light. The whole must hang together and direct our attention at once to what happened and to the meaningful dimension of what happened. A particular battle, for instance, may be described as a turning point in a war, with the benefit of retrospection and a knowledge of its long-term consequences. A turning point is a narrative fragment, not something that is isolated in time. The same can be said for the countless leadings and consequences of which historical accounts are replete: event X led to Y, which

---

[51] Ricoeur, *Time and Narrative*, vol. 1, xi.

produced consequence Z, which led to A, and so on in a story that can go on and on (one can spot the historical books on any shelf by the generous width of their spines). A fictional narrative could also go on and on and must be brought to a conclusion in a way that produces an appropriate ending – one that is determined by the logic of the narrative itself – and something similar may be said of the historical narrative. Determining the end of the story, or the end of the book, is a similar decision on the historian's part, and it is one of countless decisions the historian must make in the course of crafting – one might also say composing – a narrative. A book on the fall of the Roman Empire should properly begin in what year, and in what year does it end? Does it include the Eastern Empire? These are far from self-evident but call upon the historian to make important decisions about how the account as a whole is going to hold together into a unity – which overlaps with and otherwise relates to other unities, as one philosopher's book relates to another book by that author, and to similar books by other authors, and so on, in the nature of an organic being. Grasping relations and identifying for the reader the almost infinite interrelatedness of human events while selecting and highlighting some others all belong to the historian's task. In crafting a story they are engaging in an art that is not identical to the novelist's, but the family resemblance is unmistakable. Historians also debate, argue, demonstrate, and critique alternative accounts; they reckon with no end of facts, data, evidence, documents, and so on, but what Ricoeur was bringing to our attention is the art by which all of these are synthesized by the historian and that the work of integration is not a bit of literary window dressing applied after the fact of achieving real knowledge. Historical understanding assumes the form of a story, and to all storytelling belongs a kind of artfulness.

The mode of artfulness that the historian practices is clearly not identical to the novelist's, and I shall return to the question of what distinguishes the two in due course. First, let us take a closer look at Ricoeur's analysis of the art of what he termed "emplotment." A narrative contains a plot which integrates and moves along everything that the narrative encompasses in some identifiable direction. "Plot, says Aristotle, is the *mimēsis* of an action" or a certain kind of imitation. Ricoeur added, "I shall distinguish at least three senses of this *mimēsis*: a reference back to the familiar pre-understanding we have of the order of action; an entry into the realm of poetic composition; and finally a new configuration by means of this poetic refiguring of the pre-understood order of action." There is a good deal going on in this passage, and I shall not examine all the details of a sprawling hypothesis that Ricoeur would require three volumes of *Time and Narrative* to present. Let us concentrate on the main aspects of his account that bear directly upon historical inquiry, beginning with the first of the three senses of *mimēsis* or imitation. An historical narrative of, let us say, the assassination of Julius Caesar presents not the action itself but a *mimēsis* of it, a word that is usually translated as "imitation" or "representation" but which Ricoeur preferred to leave untranslated. Following Aristotle, Ricoeur held that a plot imitates the action, and in a sense that needs to be clarified. It does not, strictly speaking, represent or copy the action but preunderstands it in a richer way. In his words, "To imitate or represent action is first to preunderstand what human acting is, in its semantics, its symbolic system, its temporality. Upon this preunderstanding ... emplotment is constructed." Already implicit in human action are often tacit meanings, a symbolic dimension, and a temporal structure which make the action something that is capable of being understood. Before it is understood explicitly it is preunderstood on the basis of a preliminary intelligibility, as Gadamer maintained that prejudices precede and make possible all interpretation. Human action contains "an initial *readability*" which gives the historian something upon which they may get a hold. To speak of an "assassination" already conveys some initial meaning on the action we are investigating, an action with a temporal structure and which also might stand as a symbol. Intentions, actors, circumstances, and of course a victim are contained or implicit within it, as are relations to other actions, all of which give our account in a preliminary way its "aboutness" quality. The action that brought Caesar's life to an end is not devoid of intelligibility before the historian arrives upon the scene, but instead there are the makings of a story here, some intelligible elements upon which the interpreter must set to work. The larger significance of each of the elements is not understood at this stage of the interpretive process, but the point is that the historian is not confronted with a flux or a blank canvas upon which anything at all may be inscribed. Something has happened that the historian must be faithful to, so to speak, or articulate correctly. The historian's subsequent "composition of the plot is grounded in a preunderstanding of the world of action, its meaningful structures, its symbolic resources, and its temporal character."[52]

One is not, as White believed, inventing a plot in the sense of imposing it onto the events themselves but rendering explicit what is already implicit and inchoate within them. Human actions have what may be called a prenarrative quality; they are rich with symbolism, intentions and consequences, temporality, relations, norms, and everything with which a culture invests them in a given time and place. It is the nature of human action, as Ricoeur expressed it, to be "in quest of narrative," and indeed we can "speak of a human life as a story in its nascent state."[53] Historical interpretation is a narrative configuration that is

---

[52] Ibid., xi, 64, 58, 54.   [53] Ibid., 74.

based upon an initial prefiguration, or understanding sets to work on what has already been in a sense preunderstood or grasped in a preliminary way. The historian is more midwife than conjuror, and their work is to configure a narrative that emerges from events and actions which are never chaotic or devoid of significance. The activity of narrative configuration may be spoken of as an art, but it is also grounded in the things themselves. The dichotomy of art and science is an obstacle here as we are speaking of an interpretive activity that partakes of poetic composition and empirical factfinding in their mutuality. As one scholar puts it,

> Historical narratives are constrained by a demand for documentary evidence. But they are still creative. Their plots are never simply read off of events themselves, though they are prefigured by them. Even seemingly non-narrative history, such as that offered by the Annales school, involves active, poetic configuration. This does not make historical narratives fictions. "Historical knowledge," Ricoeur argues, "proceeds from our narrative understanding without losing any of its scientific ambition."[54]

Ricoeur assigned to the creative or compositional dimension of this the term "semantic innovation," and it finds its principal expression in metaphor and narrative. The latter must be crafted or configured explicitly, and again not in any way the historian likes but on the basis of what is implicit in the phenomena. The innovation here lies in the historian's creative synthesis by means of a plot that holds together the numerous elements that convey to the reader what happened, from the various actors and their intentions to names and dates, actions and consequences, plans undertaken and foiled, chance occurrences, and anything else that is relevant to the whole and moves it along from the story's beginning to end. "It is this synthesis of the heterogeneous," Ricoeur wrote, "that brings narrative close to metaphor. In both cases, the new thing – the as yet unsaid, the unwritten – springs up in language."[55] It is the nature of semantic innovation, whether in metaphor or narrative, to bring into proximity what had been disparate, to see X in light of Y or in relation to Z, and in the case of an historical narrative to weave into a (in some ways) novel configuration a nascent narrative.

The historian is an organizer of sorts. Their task is not merely to re-present in any sense that resembles replicating or saying again without addition or subtraction the contents of a chronicle (which is already a selection and an abstraction) but to arrange some large or small occurrence within historical

---

[54] Robert Piercey, "Narrative" in *The Blackwell Companion to Hermeneutics*, ed. Niall Keane and Chris Lawn (Malden: Wiley Blackwell, 2016), 176.
[55] Ricoeur, *Time and Narrative*, vol. 1, ix.

reality into an episode in a larger universality that has temporal extension. In the same philosopher's words, *"time becomes human to the extent that it is articulated through a narrative mode."*[56] The human experience of time, as Heidegger had described it, is of a pulling along toward what is next and out of a past that we are never entirely finished with (and which may not be finished with us). A narrative mode of interpretation displays the same structure as human temporality itself and so elucidates our experience by holding together the various elements that are relevant to a given historical event in a linguistic account that stretches along in time. The emplotment organizes all such elements into an arrangement that may be understood and which hangs together in the way and to the extent that anything in our experience does. An individual life also displays this basic structure, although developing this hypothesis would take us far afield. The meaning of any event, in an historical account as in an individual life, is little unto itself but consists mainly in its contribution as a particular within a larger configuration or temporal context. The assassination of Caesar was a crucial episode in the evolution of Rome from a republic to an empire, and while this is not its sole meaning it is a large part of it. It presumably would have meant rather a lot to the man himself, had he had much time to think about it, but its historical significance is much larger than this. We are operating within the hermeneutic circle here again: the meaning of an action comes into view in light of its relation to a larger universality such as a plot while the meaning of the latter is dependent upon the particulars that constitute it. Mediating between universal and particular is no straightforward undertaking but requires an organizing skill which, when it succeeds, brings about a mutual illumination between the story as a whole and the events within it.

For what reason is a given action or event deemed "historical"? What Caesar had for breakfast on the day in question is not historical, but on what grounds? The action must hold a certain significance, but the crucial point about significance which hermeneuticists point out is that this is largely if not wholly a relational value. "In itself," as it were, or when regarded as a bare particular, not much of anything in the realm of human activity holds meaning, or not much. What he had for breakfast means very little because it relates to very little, produced few if any consequences, was not much of a response to anything, and has every appearance of a dumb happening. If one were interested in the history of food, or of breakfast, of what famous or everyday Romans had for breakfast, or something similar, the event might take on historical meaning, but otherwise historians are not interested in such a matter because it is unrelated to his murder. An action gains historical significance by participating in and moving

---

[56] Ibid., 52.

along some larger train of events that takes place over time, and thus by becoming what is properly spoken of as an episode. (Gadamer would add that the significance it assumes also and importantly depends upon the questions we are asking about it.) The action already lends itself to "poetic composition," but it becomes historical in being taken up in a narrative composition. It is regarded as part of a sequence, as a reaction or an anticipation, as belonging to a trend or a pattern, or as an instance of some larger theme. Its prenarrative quality must become fully actualized in an account that highlights some factors while omitting or downplaying others, selects and arranges events into a followable order, and is presented from a particular vantage point. The larger aim of the account is to answer who, what, why, when, and where of whatever events we are recounting as well as some larger sense of what it all meant. Ricoeur was well aware that in this process "[h]istorians do argue in a formal, explicit, discursive way .... Historians have their own modes of arguing, but these belong to the narrative domain."

This point is quite important: the hermeneutical philosopher of history draws attention to the situatedness of the inquirer, understanding over explanation, emplotment, and the historical imagination, yet without going to an extreme of anti-empiricism or anti-realism. Clearly, the historical researcher is on a fact-finding mission and is constantly examining evidentiary material of one kind or another; they engage in explicit argumentation and criticism of competing accounts; they reckon with no end of facts and publish their findings in a rigorous manner. Historians may be, and typically are, as intellectually tough-minded as their colleagues in many other disciplines. Ricoeur's point is not to deny any of this but to propose that the larger picture of what historians do is to configure narratives that make a claim to truth, as the word "*historia*" already suggests. Emplotment, "poetic composition," and imaginative storytelling encompass a great part of what humanists and social scientists in general do, even as much of it occurs somewhat below the surface. Philosophers, too, are storytellers of a kind, including those for whom all that pertains to the imagination is deemed out of order. What Ricoeur spoke of as the "synthesis of the heterogeneous" belongs in a fundamental way to what minds do, and where this is understood not as an external imposition or a reading into the phenomena but a rendering explicit of what is already there. We come to understand what has been preunderstood and narrate what lends itself to the narration. As the meaning of a text "is the joint work of the text and reader," and "as Aristotle said that sensation is the common work of sensing and what is sensed," historical meaning is the "the common work" of actions and events that do not speak for themselves and the historical accounts in which they are brought into language.[57]

---

[57] Ibid., 164–165, 83, 76.

Terms like narrative (a rather overused word these days which shades all too often into sophistry and manipulation), emplotment, and "poetic composition" invite a degree of skepticism. Narrative in particular has been a much-discussed topic among historians and philosophers of history for a few decades now, and all too often the suspicion arises – justifiably in many instances – that the purveyor of a narrative has something up their sleeve and that common-sense empiricism has been sacrificed for either an ideology or some nefarious purpose. It is the truth about the human past that we are interested in after all, not aesthetics or anyone's political project. Historians are neither activists nor tellers of tales but dealers in fact. Hermeneutics does maintain this, but in order to sustain this position we must say a few words about the distinctions between historical and fictional narratives and between history and politics. What distinguishes historical from fictional narratives is less straightforward than it may appear, for we cannot claim that the fictional storyteller simply spins yarns out of nothing or makes it up without following rules that belong to their particular art. Artists too have rules and work in a tradition, and while the manner in which they follow these allows for a great deal of freedom they do not create in a vacuum. A novelist is not constrained by "what really happened," for indeed nothing happened in fact, but the way the author goes about composing the narrative must make a certain kind of sense or indeed be true in an aesthetic sense. They are constrained by the logic of the narrative itself as it goes along and may no more tack on an ending that fails to cohere with the whole than Michelangelo might have inserted a large and randomly placed purple square on the ceiling of the Sistine Chapel. It is not correct in the sense of indicated by the rest of the work and the meaning of that work. Historians are similarly limited, but they are clearly limited as well by the need to do justice to the facts and evidence that they encounter in the course of their research. An historian whose hypothesis is contradicted by a set of incontrovertible documents, let us say, is not free in the manner of the novelist to disregard it but is as beholden as any scientist to what they find. A kind of empiricism or realism rules here in the sense that historical narratives that drift far from the shore of facts (documents, artifacts, names, dates, etc.) fail, even as facts speak for themselves in only a limited way. Facts must be brought to life, rendered intelligible, and accounted for, for otherwise they are as mute as any bare particular. Historical narratives are true in a sense of the word that literary narratives are not and are beholden to some but not all of the aesthetic rules or conventions to which the latter are subject.

Regarding the distinction between history and politics, if it is the fundamental aim of historical understanding to allow the past to speak by bringing about a fusion of horizons between the interpreter and their object, political ideology is more likely to be an obstacle to this than an enabling condition. Narrating the past through the medium of an ideology will bring certain matters to light while placing others in shadow, as may be said of any interpretive standpoint. Total illumination is not possible here, yet it remains that some lights cast more shadow than light, and in the case of ideologies the pronounced tendency is to sacrifice interpretive rigor for political conviction. The historian's task is not to persuade their readers of the validity of an ideology but to recount what happened and what it can be understood to have meant – a project that will sometimes take on a political resonance, but when the resonance becomes pronounced, interpretive faithfulness places second to championing a cause.

4 The Constructivist Overcorrection and Other Developments

Historical constructivism has had many defenders over the last few decades, perhaps the most noted among whom is White whose *Metahistory* has been as influential as any text in contemporary philosophy of history. In White's formulation of the constructivist hypothesis, the narrative structure that the historian formulates is constructed and imposed upon past events rather than in any meaningful sense discovered. The historian is not as free as the novelist due to the role that evidence plays in all historical research, but the central point is that the narratives they relate are not discovered but fashioned. Events and actions of the past – the stuff of which history is made – simply happen and neither have a prenarrative quality nor lend themselves to a narrative telling. White articulated the point this way:

> It is sometimes said that the aim of the historian is to explain the past by "finding," "identifying," or "uncovering" the "stories" that lie buried in chronicles; and that the difference between "history" and "fiction" resides in the fact that the historian "finds" his stories, whereas the fiction writer "invents" his. This conception of the historian's task, however, obscures the extent to which "invention" also plays a part in the historian's operations. The same event can serve as a different kind of element of many different historical stories, depending on the role it is assigned in a specific motific characterization of the set to which it belongs. The death of the king may be a beginning, an ending, or simply a transitional event in three different stories. In the chronicle, this event is simply "there" as an element of a series; it does not "function" as a story element.[58]

It is wholly the historian's decision whether to place a particular event in one or another location in a sequence, for instance, for in reality events simply happen and are mute. It is the historian's retrospective imagination that assigns them their location and significance within a narrative.

---

[58] Hayden White, *Metahistory: The Historical Imagination in Nineteenth-Century Europe* (Baltimore: Johns Hopkins University Press, 1973), 6–7.

Louis Mink advanced the same point more concisely: "stories are not lived but told" by the historical interpreter.[59] Narrative is in every case transferred from the aesthetic domain to events themselves and in no sense belongs to them while the interpreter's selection of a narrative form is autonomous. Historians interpret events in a sense of freely constructing a meaning that is not found but supplied by the narrative form or strategy. Historical meanings, causes, and relations are all imaginative creations, and any judgments we form about the account as a whole is contingent not upon factual but aesthetic factors. In any recounting of the human past, the constructivist maintains, "anything goes." As Keith Jenkins, citing White, expresses it:

> For we could only presume that "the facts of the matter" set limits to the sorts of stories/narratives we can tell if we believe that the events themselves have in them a latent story form and a definitive, knowable plot structure. In which case – *if they did* – then we could indeed dismiss, say, a comic or pastoral story "from the ranks of competing narratives as manifestly false to the facts – or at least to the facts that matter – of the Nazi era." But of course they don't. For as White says elsewhere "one must face the fact that when it comes to apprehending the historical record, there are no grounds to be found in the historical record itself for preferring one way of construing meanings over another."

Jenkins adds, "historians are not only able to impose any narrative (substance) they like on 'the past' but they *have* to do so given that the past, however construed, has no narrative substance of its own."[60]

For the constructivist or idealist, any historical objectivism or realism is untenable. The hypothesis is differently formulated by different theorists, of course, and I shall not attempt an examination of each of these but present the basic hypothesis that constructivists from White to Jenkins and other postmodern philosophers of history defend. Any meanings, patterns, relations, or causes of which an historical account speaks are imaginatively constructed and projected onto events rather than found in the events themselves. "Because," as Jouni-Matti Kuukkanen writes, "there is no narrative structure or any other 'untold story' in the past, there is nothing to tell and nothing to discover, even if we had the 'access.' The past only becomes narratively structured through the imagination and the hand of the historian, who imposes order and meaning there."[61] Indeed

---

[59] Louis O. Mink, "History and Fiction as Modes of Comprehension," *New Literary History* 1, 557. Alasdair MacIntyre's reply to Mink – that "Stories are lived before they are told" – encapsulates the hermeneutical position. Alasdair MacIntyre, *After Virtue: A Study in Moral Theory* (Notre Dame University Press, 1981), 212.

[60] Keith Jenkins, *At the Limits of History: Essays on Theory and Practice* (New York: Routledge, 2009), 137–138, 8.

[61] Jouni-Matti Kuukkanen, *Postnarrativist Philosophy of Historiography* (New York: Palgrave Macmillan, 2015), 40.

the past itself along with its narrative ordering and relations does not exist until the historian pronounces it so. According to White, "The historical past is a theoretically motivated construction, existing only in the books and articles published by professional historians."[62] Willie Thompson formulates the constructivist hypothesis even more succinctly: "the past *is* essentially nothing other than what historians write," while for Jenkins the past is "a blank canvas or screen onto which historians can paint or project any history to suit."[63] Historical understanding is a construction, not a discovery, where the distinction is categorical. This view is an application of a broader thesis that postmodernists and many others have applied for several decades now to human experience in general. In the stronger formulation of this view that White defends, "historical interpretations are little more than projections."[64] How they are not wholly projections is somewhat elusive in White's writings; he would qualify this by writing that "the best grounds for choosing one perspective on history rather than another are ultimately aesthetic and moral rather than epistemological."[65] Anything resembling an historical epistemology is impossible, while the past itself – if indeed it exists – can only consist in the sort of matters that we read in a chronicle: now one thing, now another, arising from and leading nowhere, relating to and signifying nothing. Any such values are the historian's invention and do not admit of grounds other than the aesthetic or the moral. As Jenkins plainly puts it, "We're all relativists now," and "that's fine."[66]

Hermeneuticists are decidedly not in the relativist camp and nor are they thoroughgoing constructivists. The latter position holds to a conception of historical interpretation as a kind of violence on the historian's part, and one that the past itself is incapable of resisting. Nothing in the human past is capable of protesting the historian's creative activity or, in some formulations, can even be said to exist prior to such activity. After the linguistic and postmodern turns, historical facts and truth are largely regarded as epistemological fictions as there is nothing outside of language and texts to which historical interpretation can be faithful or unfaithful. Language can refer only to itself, while any facts or "data" can only be constructions that we mistakenly impose upon the world. There is nothing that an historian could get right or wrong. Michel Foucault and Jacques

---

[62] Cited in Robert Doran's "Editor's Introduction: Choosing the Past: Hayden White and the Philosophy of History" in *Philosophy of History after Hayden White*, ed. Robert Doran (London: Bloomsbury, 2013), 15.
[63] Willie Thompson, *Postmodernism and History* (New York: Palgrave Macmillan, 2004), 1; Jenkins, *At the Limits of History*, 4.
[64] Hayden White, "The Historical Text as Literary Artifact" in *History and Theory: Contemporary Readings*, ed. Brian Fay, Philip Pomper, and Richard T. Vann (Malden: Blackwell, 1998), 28.
[65] White, *Metahistory*, xii.   [66] Jenkins, *At the Limits of History*, 12.

Derrida are both very much in the background here, although the intellectual ancestors of this general view are legion.

The constructivist hypothesis from the point of view of philosophical hermeneutics is an overcorrection to a naive empiricism or positivist position for which historical research is essentially a fact-finding investigation where facts speak for themselves and no truck is had with the poetic, compositional, or imaginative. The model for the positivist is always natural science and a rather hard-nosed conception of science at that. Not interpretation but representation is the key concept, along with explanation, laws, cause and effect, objectivity, and so on. There is much in this stance that does not stand up to scrutiny, no doubt, but the difficulty with constructivist argumentation in its various forms is its constant tendency toward overcorrection which creates a distortion of its own. What we have called common-sense empiricism, where this signifies not a full-blown empiricist epistemology in the tradition of a Locke or a Hume but a resolutely phenomenological and indeed empirical conception of historical knowledge, does go to the heart of what historians do, but with a difference. Historical inquiry, hermeneutically conceived, is at bottom an interpretation of events in the human past, where we may speak of the events themselves in the same manner that phenomenological thinkers have long spoken of the things themselves or the phenomena as they show themselves to us. The entire realm of human action and experience, of past and present alike, is intelligible to us while also being steeped in a good deal of mystery. It is "through a glass, darkly" that we see at the best of times, and in the case of the past the glass can be very shadowy indeed. Yet it gives itself to intelligibility; why this should be so is a question that takes us far beyond the philosophy of history, but how it is so does not. How is it that the past is capable of being understood by us? We have seen a common trajectory in hermeneutical thought from Dilthey through Heidegger, Gadamer, and Ricoeur according to which history is intelligible to us because we ourselves are historical beings from the ground up, in some sense of the phrase. We participate in, belong to, and are constituted by the very thing that we are trying to understand, often unknowingly, and we succeed in taking this into our grasp under certain conditions and within certain limits, but we succeed notwithstanding. Our understanding of the past is more than a one-way construction but something resembling a dialogue with the past and a bringing into explicit narrative form something that already has an implicit prenarrative quality.

One of the more noted representatives of historical constructivism in recent years is Frank Ankersmit, and it may be useful to clarify the divergence between constructivism and hermeneutics by dwelling for a moment upon his suggestion that we "see the writing of history from the point of view of aesthetics." "Like the painter," he maintains, "the historian represents (historical) reality by giving it a meaning, through the medium of his text, that reality does not have of itself." He adds that "the vocabulary of representation, unlike the vocabulary of interpretation, does not require that the past itself have a meaning. Representation is indifferent to meaning"; also, "[m]eaning is originally representational." Originally, then, or before the historian takes up his or her pen and constructs a representation, meaning is absent and Ricoeur's talk of a prenarrative quality of human experience and of actions and events as "in quest of narrative" is an illusion. Ankersmit's comparison again is with the artist such as "the painter representing a landscape, a person, and so on."[67] What is the painter doing but creating meaning where none was before, and through the medium of an artistic representation? The historian likewise creates meaning where meaning had been absent and "seeks to make present (again) an absent past."[68] Many a constructivist seems to work with a largely tacit assumption that what Ankersmit here calls "reality ... of itself" is nothing more or less than a material being or simple matter in motion. The phenomenological philosopher of history David Carr has also noted this curious fact; there seems to be a widespread assumption among narrativists, as he writes,

> that the only true "reality" is physical reality. This is ... the basis of positivist metaphysics, but it is also one of the deeply rooted prejudices of our age. Somehow the world of physical objects in space and time, the world of what is externally observable, describable, and explainable in terms of mechanical pushes and pulls, and predictable by means of general laws, counts as reality in the primary sense.[69]

Carr himself does not presuppose this and nor do hermeneuticists. Constructivists tend to, and it is seldom clear why they would. When Thompson writes that "the past *is* essentially nothing other than what historians write," "nothing" seems to intend nothing apart from brute matter in motion, and the same can be said for Jenkins when he asserts that the past is "a blank canvas or screen onto which historians can paint or project any history to suit." Why some form of metaphysical materialism should be the default position here when what we are speaking of

---

[67] F. R Ankersmit, *History and Tropology: The Rise and Fall of Metaphor* (Berkeley: University of California Press, 1994), 107, 102.
[68] F. R. Ankersmit, *Meaning, Truth, and Reference in Historical Representation* (Ithaca: Cornell University Press, 2012), 59.
[69] David Carr, *Experience and History: Phenomenological Perspectives on the Historical World* (Oxford: Oxford University Press, 2014), 208.

is the world of human experience is a mystery but for the fact that this idea is so profoundly rooted in our modern worldview.

Let us consider Ankersmit's analogy between the historian and the artist, which is an analogy that the hermeneuticist may also find useful. When an artist such as a painter perceives a landscape or a person, are they perceiving dumb matter, let us say at time TI, and then at T2 set to work creating some humanly significant meaning, by means of a representation, which the thing "of itself" lacks? The hermeneutical position is that there is no thing "of itself" of which we can speak but a tensional unity between the interpreter and their objects, whether the interpreter be an historian, artist, or anyone else. The world that we experience, the entire domain of what Dilthey called "socio-historical life," is not a world of material being alone but of intelligible relata which we may speak of as lending themselves to human understanding. Interpretation is a rendering explicit of what already gives itself to interpretation and of what has been preunderstood; it is not a re-presenting, or a presenting again, of what had been present at some previous time but is in every case a creative showing of the phenomenon or "the thing itself," which is not the thing "of itself" or "in itself." Ankersmit's contention that "the vocabulary of interpretation ... require[s] that the past itself have a meaning" is misleading; an historical event, like the landscape or the person before the artist arrives on the scene, does not have a meaning that is wholly determinate and complete, but nor is it a blank canvas. It is intermediate between the two, a relatum which calls for an interpretation that is neither a subjectivist free-for-all nor completely objective and determinate. In historical, aesthetic, and all interpretation is an imperative to be faithful to our object and to be rigorous. A landscape painter who produces random blotches of paint on a canvas is not painting the landscape or producing art but engaging in an entirely different activity. The artist enjoys a great deal of freedom in deciding how they are going to approach their painting, but the crucial point is that their freedom here is not unlimited. They are, in a sense that is elusive but important, beholden to their object, and in a similar way the historian is also beholden to what they find. The assassination of Caesar is no blank canvas, and it does not follow that its meaning is either singular, objective, or in any way conclusive. It gives rise to thought, and a mode of thought in which the historian is not entirely sovereign.

We are back to the elusive but ineluctable question of historical truth. For the constructivist (although different theorists will formulate this differently), narrative is not of the world but of the imagination, and truth gains no hold. For hermeneuticists (who also will not all speak in one voice), narrative is at once of the imagination and of the world. There is something there, in the events themselves, in the human past, that the historian must in some sense "get right," be faithful to, or tell the truth about, and this is an obligation that the historian well understands. In no way does one make it up but one relates the story as it happened, as difficult as it is to articulate philosophically this "as it happened." Unlike the fictional storyteller, the historian must "tell the truth" both in an empirical connotation of account for all the available evidence and in a sense of configure all of this into an account that discloses some humanly significant dimension of the events one is relating, while the former is not an empiricist but relates a truth in this second sense alone. The historian's form of storytelling is more literal and empirical than the novelist's, although to speak of either as "representing" a reality that is entirely dumb, as constructivists typically do, is dubious.

Consider the historian who chooses to write a book on the collapse of the Soviet Union, although any historical event would illustrate the point I am making. How plausible is it to speak of this event, or series of events, as "of itself" (Ankersmit) without meaning, a "blank canvas" (Jenkins) wholly lacking "order and meaning" until the historian "imposes" them (Kuukkanen), and indeed as "essentially nothing other than what historians write" (Thompson)? Again, "there is no ... 'untold story' in the past, there is nothing to tell and nothing to discover" (Kuukkanen), for which reason "historians are not only able to impose any narrative (substance) they like on 'the past' but they *have* to do so" (Jenkins). What does the historian "*have* to do" here? Do they have to get the basic facts right – and if so, what is this "getting right"? If the name Gorbachev is not mentioned anywhere in the book, might this not be counted an omission, a crucial element that the historian has failed to get right? What if the dates are wrong or key events are left out? Is the Estonian declaration of independence not "key" until the historian declares it so, rather as in baseball strike three is not strike three until an umpire says so (he does say so for a reason)? For the hermeneuticist, the declaration itself is "in quest of narrative" (Ricoeur) not in a fanciful sense but where this means that the event, in a way that is elusive but decisive, is not a blank canvas. It is intelligible, bears a meaning(s) or the makings of a meaning(s), has a temporal structure, perhaps a symbolic function or a potentiality to be understood as X or Y but not likely Z. The declaration was motivated, served a purpose, bore the rudiments at least of a meaning(s), took place in time, and did not appear out of nowhere but in the context of a time and place. A long series of events led up to it and also followed upon it, and it does appear that the historian who omits any of this is missing something important. The declaration is not a brute happening, and it warrants inclusion in our narrative about the Soviet Union for assignable reasons. It moves the story along, relates in numerous ways to other events, and bears a significance which the historian is not utterly free to construct or "impose." It has the ontological status of a relatum, something whose being consists in its participation in a larger process or configuration, as a pole in a dialectic, and where it falls to the historian to describe its manner of participation or its relevance to a temporally developing narrative. There is a tensional unity here between particular and universal, event and context, knower and the known, which constructivism mistakes for a one-way projection.

When historians speak of evidence and data, discovery and findings, of what are they speaking? Neither evidence, data, nor findings have an "in itself" quality but are evidence-of-X and a finding-that-Y. The cognitive act is tied inextricably to its object, and the constructivist's error is not to highlight the creative activity of the historian but to do so in a way that loses sight of the other side of a dialectic. Historians more than occasionally proffer interpretations that in some measure fail, but what is it to fail here? Something has pushed back, as it were, and what it is that does the pushing is generally referred to as "evidence," facts, sources, what really happened, as elusive as these expressions may be. The historian is not only a storyteller but a detective of a kind, and the trail they follow does not appear to be a construction for it has a stubbornness about it which is far from conforming to the historian's will. There are many things that our historian of the Soviet Union cannot say for the plain reason that they are contradicted by the evidence. The trail one is following is there and needs to be followed not in any way but in a way that is indicated by what one finds as one goes along tracking it. As hermeneutical philosopher Jeff Mitscherling has shown in the context of aesthetics, that trail has being – he terms it "intentional being" – and one follows it in the way that the thing itself seems to require.[70] Finding and discovering are apt terms here, for the historian in sifting through evidence, selecting and arranging, arguing and critiquing, and configuring the items in a chronicle into a narrative form is fashioning an account not at will but as the account itself and the evidence that is relevant to it indicate. One follows a trail where it leads, and the configuring act is at once imaginative and beholden to what one finds.

Should we speak of rationality here, it would be better to conceive this not as an epistemology but as a set of disciplinary standards, conventions, and presuppositions by which interpretive disagreements may be mediated. Historical rationality crucially bears upon concepts like sources and evidence, facts and data, justification and truth, and is contrasted with subjectivism, myth-making, propaganda, and some related matters. Interpretation and narration are central to historical investigation, and these notions are not as tender-minded as we often believe. As phenomenologist Maurice Merleau-

---

[70] See Jeff Mitscherling, *Aesthetic Genesis: The Origin of Consciousness in the Intentional Being of Nature* (Lanham: University Press of America, 2009).

Ponty put it, "we give history its sense, but not without history offering us that sense .... [O]ur assessment of the past – even if it never reaches absolute objectivity – is never entitled to be arbitrary."[71] The untenable dichotomies that both hard-nosed empiricists and constructivists often presuppose – fact-finding versus constructing, discovering versus imagining, and so on – are better regarded as distinctions that are sometimes useful and sometimes not. Ankersmit's contention that "No representation, no past," or "the past depends for its (onto)logical status on its representation," is one-sided in a way that Merleau-Ponty's statement above is not.[72] The historical past "offer[s] us that sense," and it is this to which the constructivist is unable to do justice. Historical research is as rational as research in any other field, and to say that it makes a legitimate claim to truth does not entail that it "corresponds" to a set of wholly determinate facts but that the narrative art gathers and selects, justifies and criticizes, analyzes and synthesizes, and offers a reading of whatever evidence is available to it in a way that is faithful to the things themselves.

A couple of final issues we ought to address before concluding this brief study of History and Hermeneutics are memory, "presentism," and a cultural climate that appears increasingly hostile to the humanistic tradition from which hermeneutics emerges. In recent years a good deal of interest among historians and philosophers of history has been devoted to the nature of (especially collective) memory and its significance for the study of the past. Memory has come increasingly to be seen not as a simple matter of retaining information but as a social activity that is oriented toward purposes of the present time, and which pertain more than occasionally to politics. Presentism's characteristic tendency is to regard the past from the standpoint of its relevance and usefulness for our own era and often enough from the ideological perspective that we bring with us, in the manner of Whiggish history. Without going down the presentist road, hermeneutics does regard historical memory as a capacity and activity that again involves some imaginative configuration on our part. No mere storehouse of information, historical memory involves a selective and narrative arrangement of those episodes from our shared past that we judge worthy of being carried forward in thought in light of their ability to speak to our time and purposes while other episodes are allowed to slip away into a forgotten past. Memory not only conserves the past but goes to work on it, at the best of times in order to relate it to the present in the form of learning from it and gaining an orientation on what is happening now and on what is likely to follow upon it.

---

[71] Maurice Merleau-Ponty, *Phenomenology of Perception*, trans. Colin Smith (New York: Routledge, 2013), 475–476.

[72] F. R. Ankersmit, "'Presence' and Myth," *History and Theory* 45, no. 3 (2006), 328.

Some selective forgetting is as vital as what we elect to hold onto, and an issue this raises is the basis on which given events are duly retained in the collective memory and which are not. Toward the end of his career Ricoeur remarked, "I continue to be troubled by the unsettling spectacle offered by an excess of memory here, and an excess of forgetting elsewhere, to say nothing of the influence of commemorations and abuses of memory – and of forgetting."[73] In what does an abuse of the social memory consist, or of forgetting? Memory at the best of times not only connects us to the past but grounds us thereby and supplies an orientation to the present and future which is otherwise unavailable.

An insight from phenomenologist Hannah Arendt is of some relevance here. Her concern in *Between Past and Future* pertained to the kind of remembrance that held such importance in the ancient world, perhaps most notably throughout the Roman era. Because human actions are contingent and ultimately fleeting, she noted, the historian's task is to invest them with "some permanence and ... arrest their perishability." Human action when translated into the written word assumes a form of immortality, as Plato and Aristotle had taught that the highest things are immortal and unchanging. As she expressed it, "to 'immortalize' meant for the philosopher to dwell in the neighborhood of those things which are forever, to be there and present in a state of active attention, but without doing anything, without performance of deeds or achievement of works. Thus the proper attitude of mortals, once they had reached the neighborhood of the immortal, was actionless and even speechless contemplation." As the philosopher contemplates the truth for its own sake, the purpose of historical memory is to prevent such actions from slipping into oblivion and to understand them for what they were. This value is too often lost sight of in modern times with our ostensibly scientific preoccupation with objectivity. In her words,

> Before the rise of the modern age it was a matter of course that quiet, actionless, and selfless contemplation of the miracle of being, or of the wonder of God's creation, should also be the proper attitude for the scientist, whose curiosity about the particular had not yet parted company with the wonder before the general from which, according to the ancients, sprang philosophy.[74]

Her concern was that with the loss of tradition in the modern era, "We are in danger of forgetting, and such an oblivion ... would mean that, humanly speaking, we would deprive ourselves of one dimension, the dimension of

---

[73] Paul Ricoeur, *Memory, History, Forgetting*, trans. Kathleen Blamey and David Pellauer (Chicago: University of Chicago Press, 2006), xv.
[74] Hannah Arendt, *Between Past and Future* (New York: Penguin, 2006), 43, 47, 50.

depth in human existence. For memory and depth are the same, or rather, depth cannot be reached by man except through remembrance. It is similar with the loss of religion." The decline of tradition and religion in combination "is tantamount to the loss of the groundwork of the world, ... as though we were living and struggling with a Protean universe where everything at any moment can become almost anything else." In such a condition, we no longer inhabit a shared world where knowledge and meanings are had in common. This is the world, she believed, that had come about in the twentieth century, where the individual withdraws into an empty subjectivism. The situation throughout the Roman period was the opposite of this, where the founding of Rome assumed a veritably sacred quality, remained uppermost in the social memory, and formed the basis of all political authority. Along with this form of authority, religion itself for the Romans "literally meant *re-ligare*: to be tied back, obligated, to the enormous, almost superhuman and hence always legendary effort to lay the foundations, to build the cornerstone, to found for eternity. To be religious meant to be tied to the past."[75] It would be difficult to describe citizens of modernity as tied to the past in this or perhaps in any way, and this kind of forgetfulness, Arendt warned, is a recipe for nihilism.

The hermeneuticist might well say the same. As individual memory orients present experience, tradition orients a culture by relating it toward both a living past and a hoped-for future. In the intellectual culture of our time, the ancient humanistic tradition, to say nothing of the spiritual tradition that has long been accounted the second great pillar of Western civilization, at present finds more critics than defenders and risks being forgotten entirely in the face of such challenges. Philosophical hermeneutics itself is an outgrowth of that tradition, and its proponents are likely to warn against the kind of wholesale jettisoning that some of its critics appear to be urging. For Hegel, as Gadamer expressed it, "a people without a metaphysics would be like a temple without a sanctuary," and the same may be said of a culture without a tradition.[76] Memory is never solely an individual matter but in the case of the historical past is socially shared and takes the form of tradition. This is not a new insight and may be traced back at least as far as phenomenologist Edith Stein, who showed as far back as the 1920s that intentionality is more than occasionally a social phenomenon, whether it be remembrance, forgetting, storytelling, judging, or a great many cognitive acts.[77] Like the capacity for understanding itself, memory requires

---

[75] Ibid., 94, 95, 121.
[76] See Hans-Georg Gadamer, *Reason in the Age of Science*, trans. Frederick G. Lawrence (Cambridge, MA: MIT Press, 1983), 3.
[77] See especially her *Philosophy of Psychology and the Humanities*, trans. Mary Catharine Baseheart and Marianne Sawicki (Washington, DC: Institute of Carmelite Studies, 2000).

cultivation and is discerning, selective, and compositional in ways that tend to escape our notice. It is what Gadamer spoke of as "an essential element of the finite historical being of man," and in a way that may also be said of historical imagination.[78]

A caricature of hermeneutics (there are several) regards this general approach as the product of a tradition that many would consign more or less entirely to the past. Is hermeneutics capable of speaking to a post-humanist cultural environment, or would historians, philosophers of history, and scholars across the humanities and social sciences be well advised to move on? I would make two brief remarks here. The first is to urge some caution when intellectual fashion would have us turn the page while having an often limited knowledge of that which the new trend claims to have surpassed. A relevant case in point is provided by the resurgence of pragmatism in the philosophy of history – an approach, incidentally, that from its inception has had deep affinities with phenomenology and hermeneutics. It is worth recalling that classical pragmatism itself (in the work of C. S. Peirce, William James, John Dewey, etc.) was commonly held to have been surpassed in the middle decades of the twentieth century by the analytic philosophy that had gained hegemony in philosophy departments throughout the English-speaking world. As so often happens in the history of ideas, the pragmatists' arguments themselves had been neither refuted nor especially well understood but essentially left behind. There would be no need for a contemporary resurgence had pragmatism not been prematurely eclipsed, and it is possible that hermeneutics currently finds itself in a comparable position. Second, another contemporary development within the philosophy of history prefers to move on from the nature of historical knowledge to explore history itself on a larger timescale, and while hermeneutical thinkers to date have focussed largely upon the former, they are also capable of advancing contributions to the latter.[79] A good many of the themes with which hermeneutics has long concerned itself – from the conditions and limits of historical understanding to the possible nature of a universal history – remain operative in the general field of research into the human past and its ongoing relationship with the present.

This Element in no way exhausts what hermeneutical thinkers have had to say on the general subjects of history and the philosophy of it over the last century and a half or so. Considerations of space have forced some focus upon major figures and major themes, from the critiques of progress and of philosophy of history in the grand style to the distinction of explanation and understanding, the universality of hermeneutic reflection, historical belonging and the historian as

---

[78] Gadamer, *Truth and Method*, 14.
[79] My own *Philosophical Reflections on Antiquity: Historical Change* (Lanham: Lexington, 2020) is one such effort.

a mediator with the past, historical truth, narrative configuration and the constructivist controversy, and some others. At the heart of any philosophy of history that can be described as hermeneutical is the theme of understanding in which interpreters and the past do not stand across a divide but are, in a way that is at once decisive and elusive, held together in a kind of tensional unity. A thoroughgoing objectivism and constructivism both exhibit a one-sidedness which hermeneutics endeavours to get past, and whether one employs a vocabulary of mimesis or truth, imagination or evidence, configuration or representation, or what have you, the vital question is what makes it possible to understand the past in a way that is at once richly imaginative and empirically rigorous. The truths and meanings that come down to us are neither constructions nor wholly determinate in their being but something intermediate and unitive in a way that hermeneuticists speak of as belonging. We comprehend, actively and creatively, a past to which we are also beholden, and if we may continue to maintain that there is a past that is capable of being known "as it really was," this "as it was" remains a relatum that is intelligible only from the horizon of the present.

Bibliography

Ankersmit, Frank R. *History and Tropology: The Rise and Fall of Metaphor.* Berkeley: University of California Press, 2021.

Ankersmit, Frank R. *Meaning, Truth, and Reference in Historical Representation.* Ithaca: Cornell University Press, 2012.

Ankersmit, Frank R. "'Presence' and Myth." *History and Theory* 45, no. 3. 2006.

Arendt, Hannah. *Between Past and Future.* New York: Penguin, 2006.

Babich, Babette. Ed. *Hermeneutic Philosophies of Social Science.* Berlin: de Gruyter, 2019.

Bambach, Charles R. *Heidegger, Dilthey, and the Crisis of Historicism.* Ithaca: Cornell University Press, 1995.

Barraclough, Geoffrey. "Universal History." In *Approaches to History.* Ed. H. P. R. Finberg. Toronto: University of Toronto Press, 1962, 83–110.

Beiser, Frederick C. *The German Historicist Tradition.* Oxford: Oxford University Press, 2011.

Bevir, Mark. "Historicism and the Human Sciences in Victorian Britain." In *Historicism and the Human Sciences in Victorian Britain.* Ed. Mark Bevir. Cambridge: Cambridge University Press, 2017, 1–20.

Carr, David. *Experience and History: Phenomenological Perspectives on the Historical World.* Oxford: Oxford University Press, 2014.

Carr, David. *Time, Narrative, and History.* Bloomington: Indiana University Press, 1991.

Collingwood, R. G. *The Idea of History.* Oxford: Oxford University Press, 1956.

Dilthey, Wilhelm. *Hermeneutics and the Study of History.* Ed. Rudolf Makkreel and Frithjof Rodi. Trans. Patricia Van Tuyl et al. Princeton: Princeton University Press, 1996.

Dilthey, Wilhelm. *Introduction to the Human Sciences.* Ed. Rudolf Makkreel and Frithjof Rodi. Trans. Michael Neville. Princeton: Princeton University Press, 1989.

Dilthey, Wilhelm., "The Rise of Hermeneutics." In *The Hermeneutical Tradition from Ast to Ricoeur.* Ed. Gayle L. Ormiston and Alan Schrift. Albany: State University of New York Press, 1990, 101–114.

Doran, Robert. "Editor's Introduction: Choosing the Past: Hayden White and the Philosophy of History." In *Philosophy of History after Hayden White.* Ed. Robert Doran. London: Bloomsbury, 2013, 1–34.

Bibliography 61

Droysen, Johann G. *Outline of the Principles of History.* Madrid: Hardpress, 2013.

Fairfield, Paul. *Historical Imagination: Hermeneutics and Cultural Narrative.* Lanham: Rowman and Littlefield, 2022.

Fairfield, Paul. *Philosophical Reflections on Antiquity: Historical Change.* Lanham: Lexington, 2020.

Fay, Brian, Philip Pomper, and Richard T. Vann. Eds. *History and Theory: Contemporary Readings.* Malden: Blackwell, 1998.

Figal, Günter. *Objectivity: The Hermeneutical and Philosophy.* Albany: State University of New York Press, 2010.

Gadamer, Hans-Georg. *Philosophical Hermeneutics.* Ed. and Trans. David E. Linge. Berkeley: University of California Press, 1977.

Gadamer, Hans-Georg. *Reason in the Age of Science.* Trans. Frederick G. Lawrence. Cambridge, MA: MIT Press, 1983.

Gadamer, Hans-Georg. *Truth and Method.* Second revised ed. Trans. Joel Weinsheimer and Donald G. Marshall. New York: Continuum, 1996.

Gardner, Philip. *Hermeneutics, History, and Memory.* London: Routledge, 2010.

Geertz, Clifford. *The Interpretation of Cultures.* New York: Basic Books, 1973.

Grondin, Jean. *Introduction to Philosophical Hermeneutics.* New Haven: Yale University Press, 1994.

Hardy, Barbara. "Towards a Poetics of Fiction: An Approach through Narrative." *Novel: A Forum on Fiction* 2, no. 1. Autumn 1968.

Hegel, Georg Wilhelm Friedrich. *Lectures on the Philosophy of History.* Trans. J. Sibree. New York: Dover, 2004.

Heidegger, Martin. *Being and Time.* Trans. Joan Stambaugh. Albany: State University of New York Press, 2010.

Heidegger, Martin. *Ontology – The Hermeneutics of Facticity.* Trans. John Van Buren. Bloomington: Indiana University Press, 1999.

Hutton, Patrick. *History as an Art of Memory.* Lebanon: University Press of New England, 1993.

Jenkins, Keith. *At the Limits of History: Essays on Theory and Practice.* New York: Routledge, 2009.

Keane, Niall and Chris Lawn. Eds. *The Blackwell Companion to Hermeneutics.* Chichester: Wiley Blackwell, 2016.

Kearney, Richard. *On Stories.* London: Routledge, 2001.

Kuukkanen, Jouni-Matti. *Postnarrativist Philosophy of Historiography.* New York: Palgrave Macmillan, 2015.

MacIntyre, Alasdair. *After Virtue: A Study in Moral Theory.* Notre Dame: Notre Dame University Press, 1981.

Madison, Gary B. *The Hermeneutics of Postmodernity: Figures and Themes*. Bloomington: Indiana University Press, 1989.

Madison, Gary B. "On the Importance of Getting Things Straight." In *Hermeneutic Philosophies of Social Science*. Ed. Babette Babich. Berlin: de Gruyter, 2019, 189–198.

Malpas, Jeff and Hans-Helmuth Gander. Eds. *The Routledge Companion to Hermeneutics*. New York: Routledge, 2017.

Merleau-Ponty, Maurice. *Phenomenology of Perception*. Trans. Colin Smith. New York: Routledge, 2013.

Mink, Louis O. "History and Fiction as Modes of Comprehension." *New Literary History* 1, 1970, 541–558.

Mitscherling, Jeff. *Aesthetic Genesis: The Origin of Consciousness in the Intentional Being of Nature*. Lanham: University Press of America, 2009.

Palmer, Richard E. *Hermeneutics*. Evanston: Northwestern University Press, 1969.

Piercey, Robert. "Narrative." In *The Blackwell Companion to Hermeneutics*. Ed. Niall Keane and Chris Lawn. Malden: Wiley Blackwell, 2016, 172–179.

Ricoeur, Paul. *Memory, History, Forgetting*. Trans. Kathleen Blamey and David Pellauer. Chicago: University of Chicago Press, 2006.

Ricoeur, Paul. *Time and Narrative*. Vols. 1–3. Chicago: University of Chicago Press, 1985–88.

Stein, Edith. *Philosophy of Psychology and the Humanities*. Trans. Mary Catharine Baseheart and Marianne Sawicki. Washington, DC: Institute of Carmelite Studies, 2000.

Thompson, Willie. *Postmodernism and History*. New York: Palgrave Macmillan, 2004.

Tucker, Alviezer. *Our Knowledge of the Past: A Philosophy of Historiography*. Cambridge: Cambridge University Press, 2009.

White, Hayden. *The Content of the Form: Narrative Discourse and Historical Representation*. Baltimore: Johns Hopkins University Press, 1990.

White, Hayden. "The Historical Text as Literary Artifact." In *History and Theory: Contemporary Readings*. Ed. Brian Fay, Philip Pomper, and Richard T. Vann. Malden: Blackwell, 1998, 1–12.

White, Hayden. *Metahistory: The Historical Imagination in Nineteenth-Century Europe*. Baltimore: Johns Hopkins University Press, 1975.

For Gwyneth

Cambridge Elements

Historical Theory and Practice

Daniel Woolf
Queen's University, Ontario

Daniel Woolf is Professor of History at Queen's University, where he served for ten years as Principal and Vice-Chancellor, and has held academic appointments at a number of Canadian universities. He is the author or editor of several books and articles on the history of historical thought and writing, and on early modern British intellectual history, including most recently *A Concise History of History* (CUP 2019). He is a Fellow of the Royal Historical Society, the Royal Society of Canada, and the Society of Antiquaries of London. He is married with three adult children.

Editorial Board
Dipesh Chakrabarty, *University of Chicago*
Marnie Hughes-Warrington, *University of South Australia*
Ludmilla Jordanova, *University of Durham*
Angela McCarthy, *University of Otago*
María Inés Mudrovcic, *Universidad Nacional de Comahue*
Herman Paul, *Leiden University*
Stefan Tanaka, *University of California, San Diego*
Richard Ashby Wilson, *University of Connecticut*

About the Series
Cambridge Elements in Historical Theory and Practice is a series intended for a wide range of students, scholars, and others whose interests involve engagement with the past. Topics include the theoretical, ethical, and philosophical issues involved in doing history, the interconnections between history and other disciplines and questions of method, and the application of historical knowledge to contemporary global and social issues such as climate change, reconciliation and justice, heritage, and identity politics.

Cambridge Elements=

Historical Theory and Practice

Elements in the Series

The Fabric of Historical Time
Zoltán Boldizsár Simon and Marek Tamm

Writing the History of Global Slavery
Trevor Burnard

Plural Pasts: Historiography between Events and Structures
Arthur Alfaix Assis

The History of Knowledge
Johan Östling and David Larsson Heidenblad

Conceptualizing the History of the Present Time
María Inés Mudrovcic

Writing the History of the African Diaspora
Toyin Falola

Dealing with Dark Pasts: A European History of Auto-Critical Memory in Global Perspective
Itay Lotem

A Human Rights View of the Past
Antoon De Baets

Historians' Autobiographies as Historiographical Inquiry: A Global Perspective
Jaume Aurell

Historiographic Reasoning
Aviezer Tucker

Pragmatism and Historical Representation
Serge Grigoriev

History and Hermeneutics
Paul Fairfield

A full series listing is available at: www.cambridge.org/EHTP

For EU product safety concerns, contact us at Calle de José Abascal, 56–1°,
28003 Madrid, Spain or eugpsr@cambridge.org.

www.ingramcontent.com/pod-product-compliance
Lightning Source LLC
LaVergne TN
LVHW020352260326
834688LV00045B/1677